Now thanks be to God who always leads us in triumph…
2 Corinthians 2:14

Most Strang Communications/Charisma House/Christian Life/Excel Books/FrontLine/Realms/Siloam products are available at special quantity discounts for bulk purchase for sales promotions, premiums, fund-raising, and educational needs. For details, write Strang Communications/Charisma House/Christian Life/Excel Books/FrontLine/Realms/Siloam, 600 Rinehart Road, Lake Mary, Florida 32746, or telephone (407) 333-0600.

But God by Phil Pringle
Published by Christian Life
A Strang Company
600 Rinehart Road
Lake Mary, Florida 32746
www.strangdirect.com

This book or parts thereof may not be reproduced in any form, stored in a retrieval system, or transmitted in any form by any means—electronic, mechanical, photocopy, recording, or otherwise—without prior written permission of the publisher, except as provided by United States of America copyright law.

Unless otherwise noted, all Scripture quotations are from the New King James Version of the Bible. Copyright © 1979, 1980, 1982 by Thomas Nelson, Inc., publishers. Used by permission.

Scripture quotations marked AMP are from the Amplified Bible. Old Testament copyright © 1965, 1987 by the Zondervan Corporation. The Amplified New Testament copyright © 1954, 1958, 1987 by the Lockman Foundation. Used by permission.

Scripture quotations marked GNT are from *Good News Translation*, second edition. Copyright © 1992 by American Bible Society. Used by permission.

Scripture quotations marked KJV are from the King James Version of the Bible.

Scripture quotations marked The Message are from *The Message: The Bible in Contemporary English*, copyright © 1993, 1994, 1995, 1996, 2000, 2001, 2002. Used by permission of NavPress Publishing Group.

Scripture quotations marked NIV are from the Holy Bible, New International Version of the Bible. Copyright © 1973, 1978, 1984, International Bible Society. Used by permission.

Scripture quotations marked NLT are from the Holy Bible, New Living Translation, copyright © 1996. Used by permission of Tyndale House Publishers, Inc., Wheaton, IL 60189. All rights reserved.

Scripture quotations marked TLB are from The Living Bible. Copyright © 1971. Used by permission of Tyndale House Publishers, Inc., Wheaton, IL 60189. All rights reserved.

Cover Design and Layout by Velvet Creative. www.velvet.com.au

Copyright © 2007, 2008 by Phil Pringle. All rights reserved
This book was previously published by Pax Ministries Pty Ltd.

Library of Congress Control Number: 2008932406
International Standard Book Number: 978-1-59979-367-2

08 09 10 11 12 — 9 8 7 6 5 4 3 2 1
Printed in China

BUT GOD

PHIL PRINGLE

Introduction: "But God"	7
1. When Christ Died on the Cross	17
2. When Friends and Family Leave You	27
3. When You're Feeling Attacked	33
4. When Health Goes and Sickness Comes	39
5. When People Treat You Unjustly	45
6. When Family Turns on You	49
7. When You're Persecuted for Your Faith	55
8. When You Need God's Love	61
9. When Religion Doesn't Work	67
10. When You Have More Problems Than You Can Handle	73
11. When You're Feeling Discouraged	81
12. When You Feel Distant From God	87
13. When Your Own Mistakes Threaten to Destroy You	91
14. When You Face Enormous Opposition	97
15. When Temptation Threatens	101
16. When People Want to Get Rid of You	105
17. When You Get Yourself Into a Mess	113
18. When Your World Is Flooded	117
19. When Your Children Are in Danger	121

contents

20.	When You're Surrounded by Enemies	125
21.	When You Feel Like You're Going Down in Flames	129
22.	When the Devil Is on the Prowl	135
23.	When It's a Matter of Life and Death	141
24.	When People Deny God	147
25.	When You Feel Alone	151
26.	When People Scheme Against You	155
27.	When a Leader Tries to Destroy You	159
28.	When You Can't Interpret What's Going on in Your Life	163
29.	When You're Unsure of the Right Decision to Make	167
30.	When People With Power Attack You	171
31.	When Cruel People Prey on Your Life	175
32.	When Everyone Around Us Is Falling	179
33.	When You've Done Wrong	185
34.	When Your Family Feels the Heat	189
35.	When You're Facing Enormous Problems	193
36.	When People Curse You	199
37.	When You're Fearful	205
38.	When You're Vulnerable	209

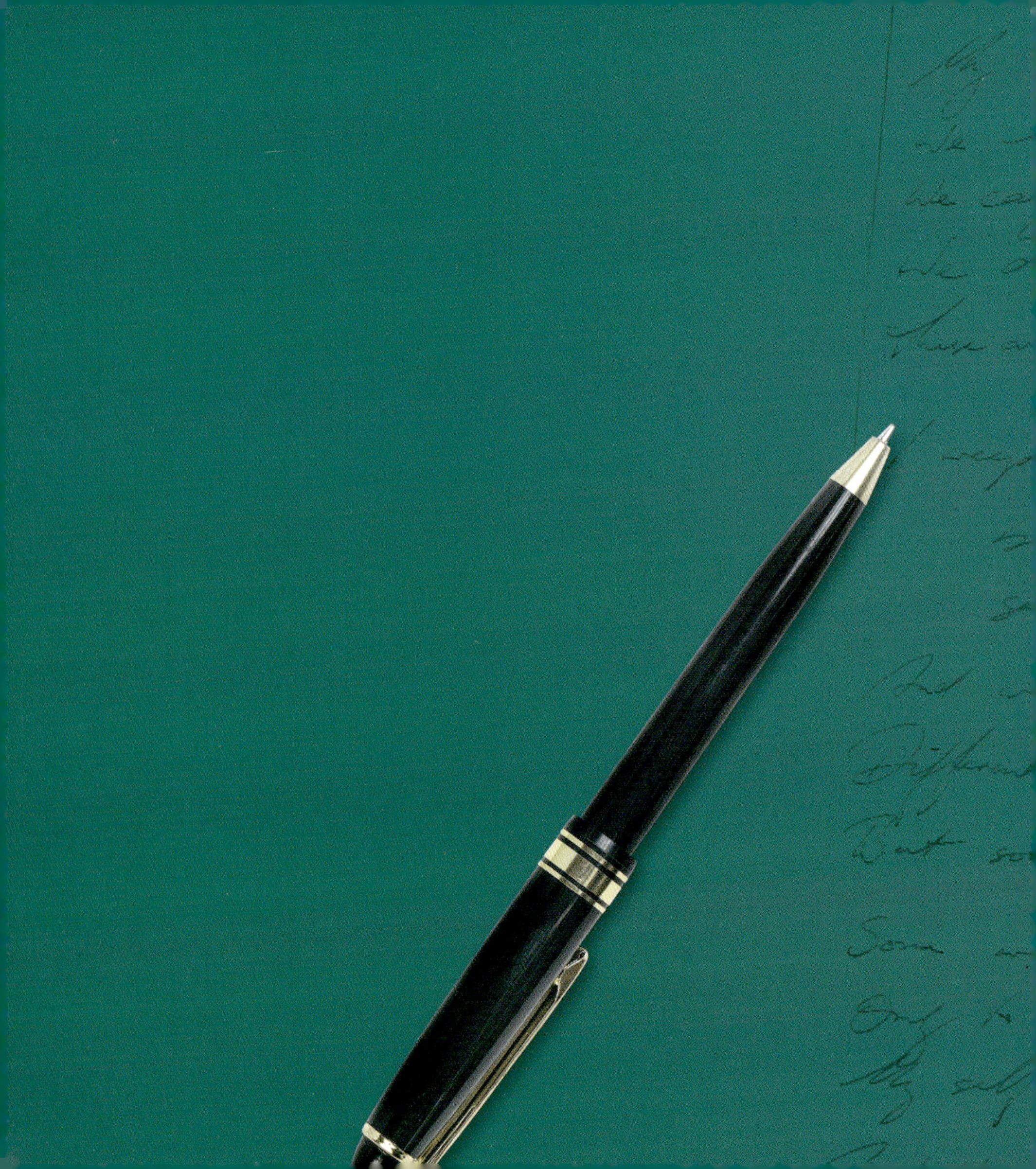

intro.

BUT GOD...

Again and again, history reveals God entering into our world and making our "impossible" situations possible. Over and over, the phrase **"but God"** appears in the Bible, confirming that God never deserts us, He overcomes our shortcomings, produces victory from defeat, and unveils Himself to His faithful ones in ways we could never even imagine.

This same God will help you and me, and all we have to do is ask Him!

"Yes, I will help you" (Isa. 41:10).

God is bigger than any problem you or I will ever face.

"He who is in you is greater than he who is in the world" (1 John 4:4).

Don't blame God for problems. Ask Him for solutions. God does incredible things when we simply ask Him.

John Wesley said, "God does nothing but in answer to prayer."

When problems get big, God can seem small. When things go bad, we often wonder why God let them happen. Bad things sometimes just happen in life. **BUT GOD** is able to reverse them and bring good out of bad.

When our problems seem impossible, panic can torment us. We can forget that God can do the impossible.

Jeremiah 2:32 says, "My people forget me" (THE MESSAGE).

When problems hijack your faith, it's easy to believe they are more powerful than your God.

Isaiah 51:13 says, "You've forgotten me, God, who made you" (THE MESSAGE).

When you come to the end of yourself and have nothing left, you might think, "God has forgotten me and has left me."

The sheer weight of a problem can overwhelm our faith. If we focus on the problem, anxiety and fear come and faith disappears. But if we make the right choices, we make the opposite take place. We collapse our problems with faith.

Faith is a feeling. It's a mind-set, a spiritual emotion. That feeling changes our personal world, and when we hold to that feeling, refusing to lose it, we position ourselves in the world of miracles.

Nehemiah 4:14 says, **"Don't be afraid! Remember the Lord who is great and glorious; fight for your families and your homes!"** (TLB).

We lose faith when we focus on the problem rather than on God. What are you thinking about—God's answers and promises, or the problem itself?

Negative situations shout for our attention, but we choose to think on the answers rather than on the problems. It's a decision we make—the decision to have faith in God and to believe that the problem will work out.

"Have faith in God" (Mark 11:22).

The time to remember God is not when it's easy, but when it's hard and we're facing an impossible problem.

"Thanks be unto God, which always causeth us to triumph" (2 Cor. 2:14, KJV).

It is God who is your Maker.

He created you.

There is no problem you face that He is unable to solve.

Isaiah 42:5 says, "Thus says God the LORD, who created the heavens and stretched them out."

There is no power more powerful than God governing the universe.

If He can create a universe without end, stars, galaxies, and a solar system, He is able to solve the problem you are facing. It is God who stretched out the heavens. It is God who created the earth and all that is in it.

Isaiah 42:5 continues, "Who spread forth the earth and that which comes from it."

There is no resource unavailable to Him, nor is there anything He cannot create to help you.

Isaiah 51:13 tell us, "The Lord your Maker, who stretched out the heavens and laid the foundations of the earth."

You may have caused the problem yourself and feel that you don't deserve His help. That's what mercy is all about—helping you get out of the mess you've made. He knows you're guilty. You know you're guilty. Everyone else knows you're guilty. **BUT GOD** always offers forgiveness.

Remember what the psalmist said? "If You, Lord, should mark iniquities, O Lord, who could stand? But there is forgiveness with You" (Ps. 130:3–4).

His mercy endures forever! No sin is greater than His mercy. No guilt can overwhelm His forgiveness. His peace is more powerful than guilty torment.

"For His mercy endures forever"

(1 Chron. 16:34).

There's the **money factor.**

There's the **guilt factor.**

There's the **people factor.**

There's the **employment factor.**

There's the **past factor.**

There's the **medical factor.**

There's the **relationship factor.**

BUT don't forget the God factor!

Remember the Lord. He's alive! Think about Him instead of the problem, and your problem will soon be buried.

"I will triumph in the works of Your hands" (Ps. 92:4).

Remember, there is no problem you will ever face that is bigger than the God who lives inside of you.

First John 4:4 says, "Greater is he that is in you, than he that is in the world" (KJV).

Bad days are inevitable. Paul even talks of an evil day (Eph. 6:13).

On those days, the devil tries to destroy us.

On those days, people attack us.

Others try to take advantage of us.

Friends may disappoint us.

Disease may try to kill us.

Enemies rise against us.

The difference is that if you have asked Christ into your life, He is in you. And His presence is the assurance of a better day, a solved problem, a transformed situation.

Colossians 1:27 reminds us, "Christ in you, the hope of glory."

No problem we face can bring us down, because we have the God factor in our lives.

Throughout Scripture, the words *but God* appear more than sixty times!

When you're facing impossible circumstances, remember

BUT GOD!

...and know that you are not on your own!

"Fear not, for I am with you" (Isa. 41:10).

"When you pass through the waters, I will be with you" (Isa. 43:2).

The forces of darkness, the enemies of God, the judgments of God, the problems of life, the storms of life—all of these threaten at some stage to take us out of the race.

There are even situations recorded in the Bible when people looked like they were finished...**BUT GOD** intervened, overwhelmed the enemy, solved the problem, and secured victory.

The greatest example in history was when all the odds were against Him...**BUT GOD** brought Jesus Christ back from the dead, resurrected with a new, eternal body, never to die again.

1.

WHEN CHRIST DIED ON THE CROSS

THEY put Jesus to death...
BUT GOD
raised Him back to life!

Three times in the Book of Acts, the writer, Luke, lets us know that no matter what people tried to do to Jesus, **God had a different plan.**

"You rejected this holy, righteous one and instead demanded the release of a murderer. You killed the author of life, **BUT GOD** raised him from the dead."
(Acts 3:14–15, NLT)

"And we apostles are witnesses of all he did throughout Judea and in Jerusalem. They put him to death by hanging him on a cross, **BUT GOD** raised him to life on the third day"
(Acts 10:39–40, NLT).

"When they had fulfilled all the prophecies concerning his death, he was taken from the cross and placed in a tomb. **BUT GOD** brought him back to life again"
(Acts 13:29–31, TLB).

icero calls crucifixion "the most cruel and disgusting penalty."

Will Durant wrote, "Even the Romans...pitied the victims."

Jewish historian Flavius Josephus observed many crucifixions and referred to them as "the most wretched of deaths."

After the verdict, the accused was tied to a post and whipped. Third-century historian Eusebius wrote of crucifixion, "The sufferer's veins were laid bare, and the very muscles, sinews, and bowels were open to exposure."

In "A Physician Testifies About the Crucifixion," Dr. C. Truman Davis writes, "The skin of the back is hanging in long ribbons and the entire area is an unrecognizable mass of torn, bleeding tissue. When it is determined by the centurion in charge that the prisoner is near death, the beating is finally stopped."

Picture this: A crown of thorns is placed on the condemned man's head. He is mocked, spat upon, beaten with a rod, and then forced to carry his crossbar to the place of his crucifixion.

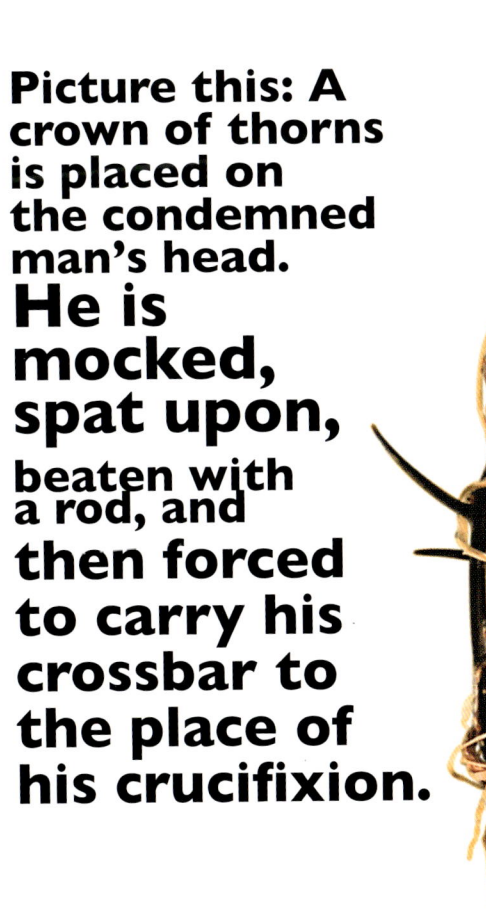

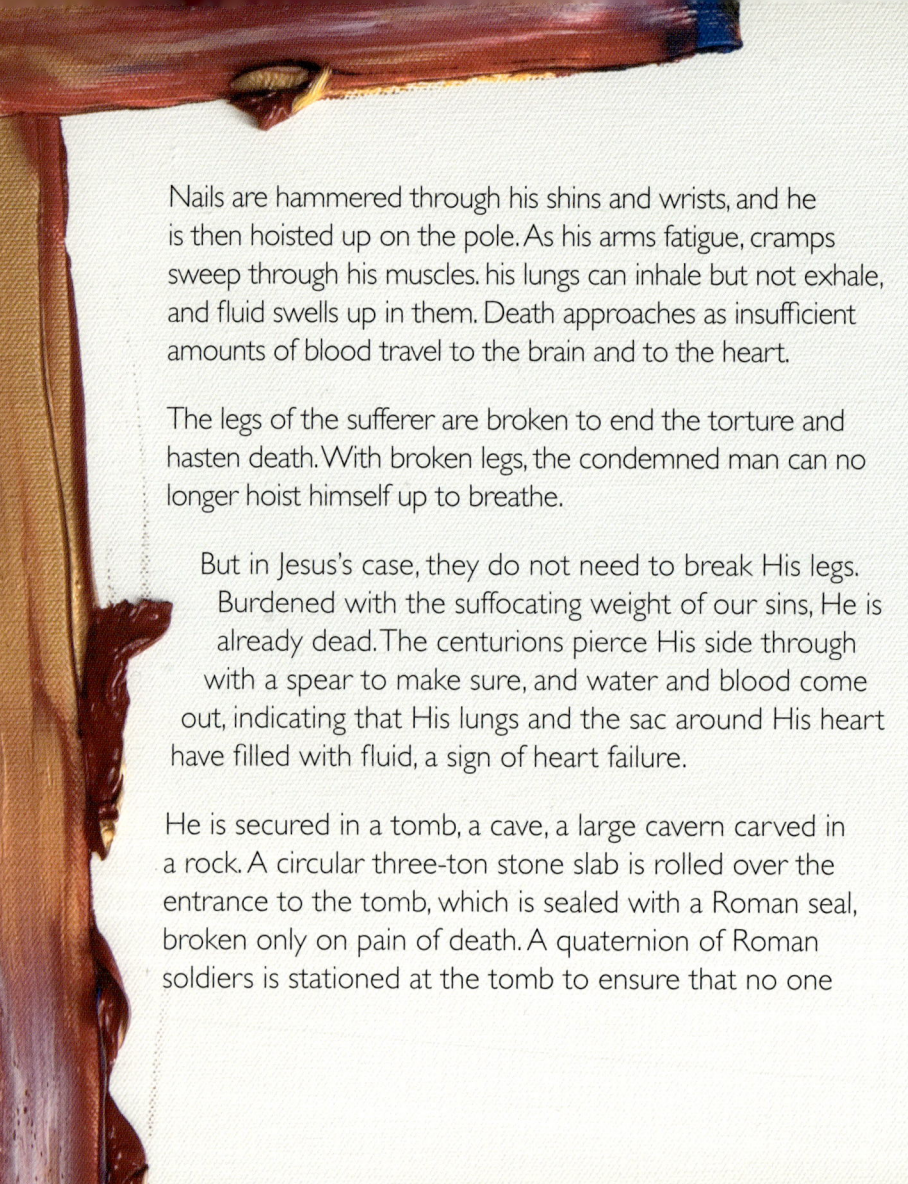

Nails are hammered through his shins and wrists, and he is then hoisted up on the pole. As his arms fatigue, cramps sweep through his muscles. his lungs can inhale but not exhale, and fluid swells up in them. Death approaches as insufficient amounts of blood travel to the brain and to the heart.

The legs of the sufferer are broken to end the torture and hasten death. With broken legs, the condemned man can no longer hoist himself up to breathe.

But in Jesus's case, they do not need to break His legs. Burdened with the suffocating weight of our sins, He is already dead. The centurions pierce His side through with a spear to make sure, and water and blood come out, indicating that His lungs and the sac around His heart have filled with fluid, a sign of heart failure.

He is secured in a tomb, a cave, a large cavern carved in a rock. A circular three-ton stone slab is rolled over the entrance to the tomb, which is sealed with a Roman seal, broken only on pain of death. A quaternion of Roman soldiers is stationed at the tomb to ensure that no one steals the body. They will be executed if they fall asleep or are slack on duty. These are the men who guard the tomb—the cruelest, strongest warriors on Earth at the time.

...BUT GOD
raises Jesus from the dead!

> It wasn't a positive attitude.

> It wasn't science or medicine.

> It wasn't people helping out.

> It was God Himself making something happen that was completely impossible.

No matter how impossible the circumstances were, no matter how many obstacles men placed in the way, no matter how many measures people took to secure the death, burial, and annihilation of Jesus, nothing could stop God from raising His Son from the dead. They hadn't counted on the God factor in Jesus's life.

This same God is in your life. The same God who raised Jesus Christ from the dead lives in you. There is no situation able to prevent God from doing what He has planned in your life.

2. WHEN FRIENDS AND FAMILY LEAVE YOU

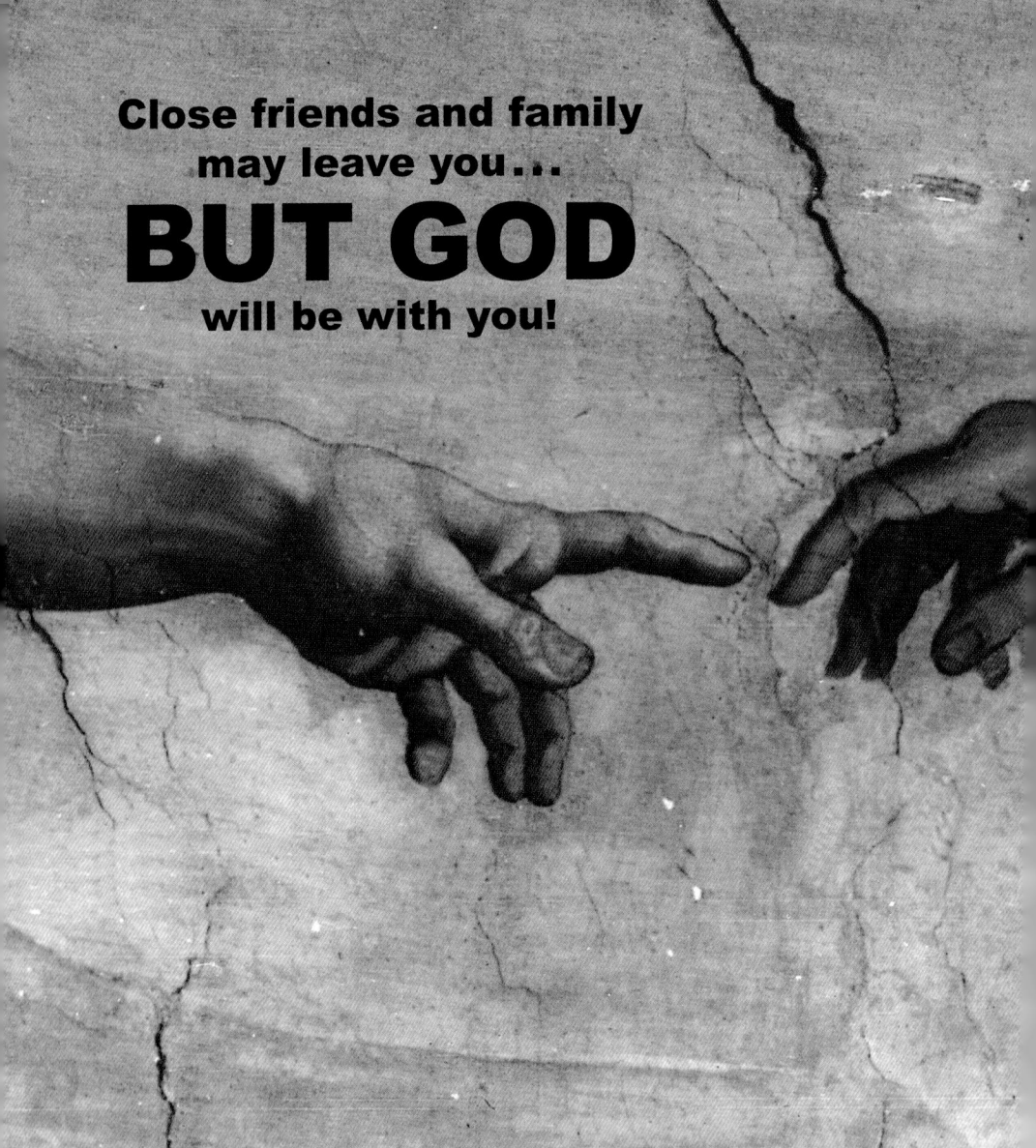

When Jacob was about to die, he assured his son Joseph that no matter happened to him, God would be with him.

"Then Jacob said to Joseph, 'Look, I am about to die, **BUT GOD** will be with you and will take you back to Canaan'" (Gen. 48:21, NLT).

God had promised to give Jacob and his children a special land, and Joseph feared that the promise would not come to pass if Jacob were gone. After all, this was the man who had seen God face to face, the man who had "wrestled" with God Himself!

But Jacob assured his son that everything was OK. "I am about to die, **BUT GOD** will be with you."

We can have the same confidence. We may have been dependent on close family and friends. They may have been the people closest to us, so we feel isolated and forsaken when they leave…

…BUT GOD will be with us!

You and I will face times when the people we love and depend upon leave us. We can't imagine surviving without them. **We will feel alone, as our closest friends, our husband, our wife, our strongest supporters and family members are no longer there for us…**

BUT GOD
will never desert us!

Joseph remembered his father's words—"I am about to die, **BUT GOD** will be with you"—and repeated them to his family when he was about to die.

"'Soon I will die,' Joseph told his brothers, '**BUT GOD** will surely come to help you and lead you out of this land of Egypt'" (Gen. 50:24, NLT).

Joseph now believed the promise of God was sure, even without help from people. Even though he was dying, he knew the promise of God would still come to pass, and he comforted those he left behind with those promises.

David the psalmist knew this truth. He knew that in the worst of times, even in the valley of the shadow of death, "You are with me" (Ps. 23:4). God will never leave us or forsake us. The Amplified Bible says it like this:

"He [God] Himself has said, I will not in any way fail you nor give you up nor leave you without support. [I will] not, [I will] not, [I will] not in any degree leave you helpless nor forsake nor let [you] down (relax My hold on you)! [Assuredly not!]" (Heb. 13:5).

Your friends, your family, your closest loved ones may leave you… **BUT GOD** will never forsake you!

3. WHEN YOU'RE FEELING ATTACKED

David learned this firsthand when he was still just a boy.

"David now stayed in the strongholds of the wilderness and in the hill country of Ziph. Saul hunted him day after day, **BUT GOD** didn't let Saul find him" (1 Sam. 23:14, NLT).

Young David had been selected by Samuel, prophet and kingmaker, to be the next king of Israel while King Saul was still alive. Saul had grown to hate David—and he wanted him dead. Saul had all the might of the Israeli army behind him, but David had nothing, so he simply hid himself in the desert. The king hunted for David every day, trying to find him to kill him…**BUT GOD** wouldn't let him be found!

"For strangers are attacking me; violent people are trying to kill me. They care nothing for God. **BUT GOD** is my helper. The Lord keeps me alive!" (Ps. 54:3–4, NLT).

Day and night David was a fugitive, living on the edge of his nerves, trying to avoid Saul and his army as they searched everywhere for him. They were constantly unsuccessful because God kept frustrating their plans, hiding David from them.

You too may feel attacked... BUT GOD will protect you!

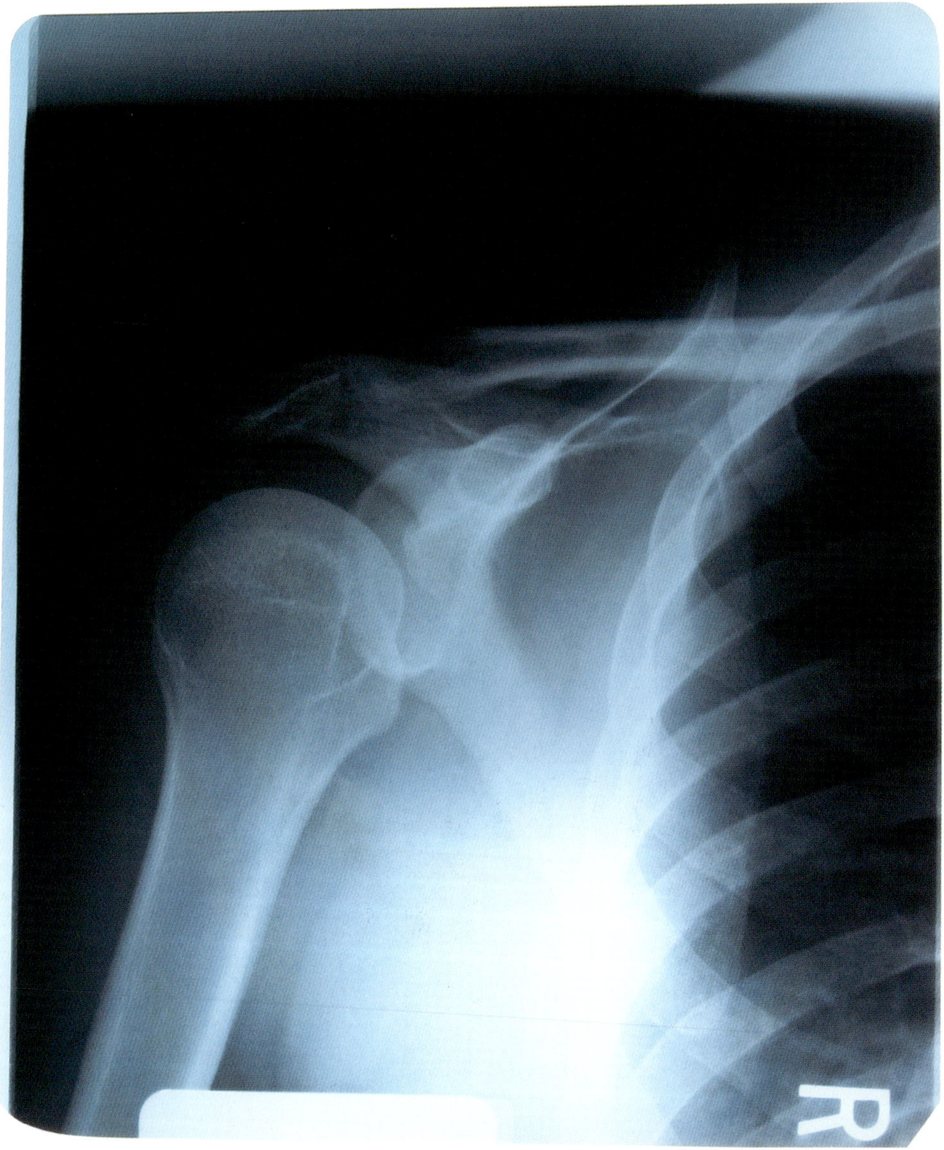
R

4. WHEN HEALTH GOES AND SICKNESS COMES

Sickness may come into your life and the those of your loved ones…

BUT GOD brings healing.

The writer of Psalm 73:26 knew this truth well. He wrote, "My health may fail, and my spirit may grow weak, **BUT GOD** remains the strength of my heart" (NLT).

I may be unable to do much because of my health…
My determination and inner strength grow weak because of all the pressure…
I can't always do all I want to make it through…

BUT GOD will make up for any lack!

He will

He will be the strength of my heart.
He will help me believe when I cannot.
He will help me love when I have no more to give.
He will be all I'm meant to be when I find I have nothing left within me

Philippians 2:27 says, "And he [Epaphroditus] certainly was ill; in fact, he almost died. **BUT GOD** had mercy on him" (NLT).

Epaphroditus was deathly sick… **BUT GOD** healed him. Thousands of times throughout the Bible, God healed the sick.

God doesn't always prevent bad things from happening, but when they do happen, He can reverse it. Just because we serve God, and even if we are as prayerful as Epaphroditus was, it doesn't mean that bad things won't happen. Epaphroditus was a man of faith, deeply devoted to prayer—and yet he still became sick.

BUT GOD brought him healing. Whatever illness we have, God can heal it. He gives us healing through the work of His Son on the cross. If we will look to Christ as our first call for healing, rather than making anything else that first call, we will find healing. If we call on God, the Bible promises healing. It's that simple.

Your health may fail and your strength may wane…
BUT GOD is the health of your life!

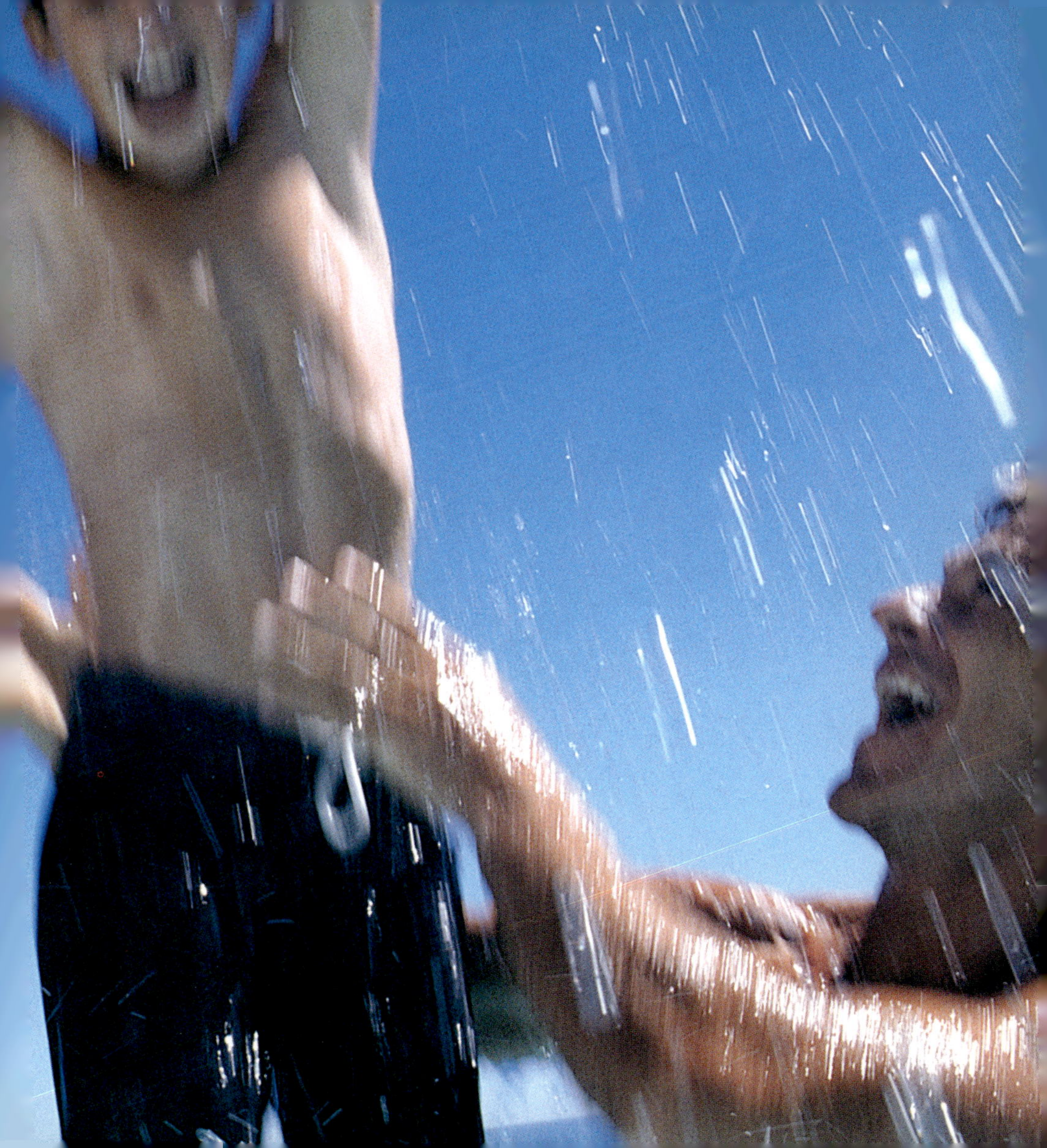

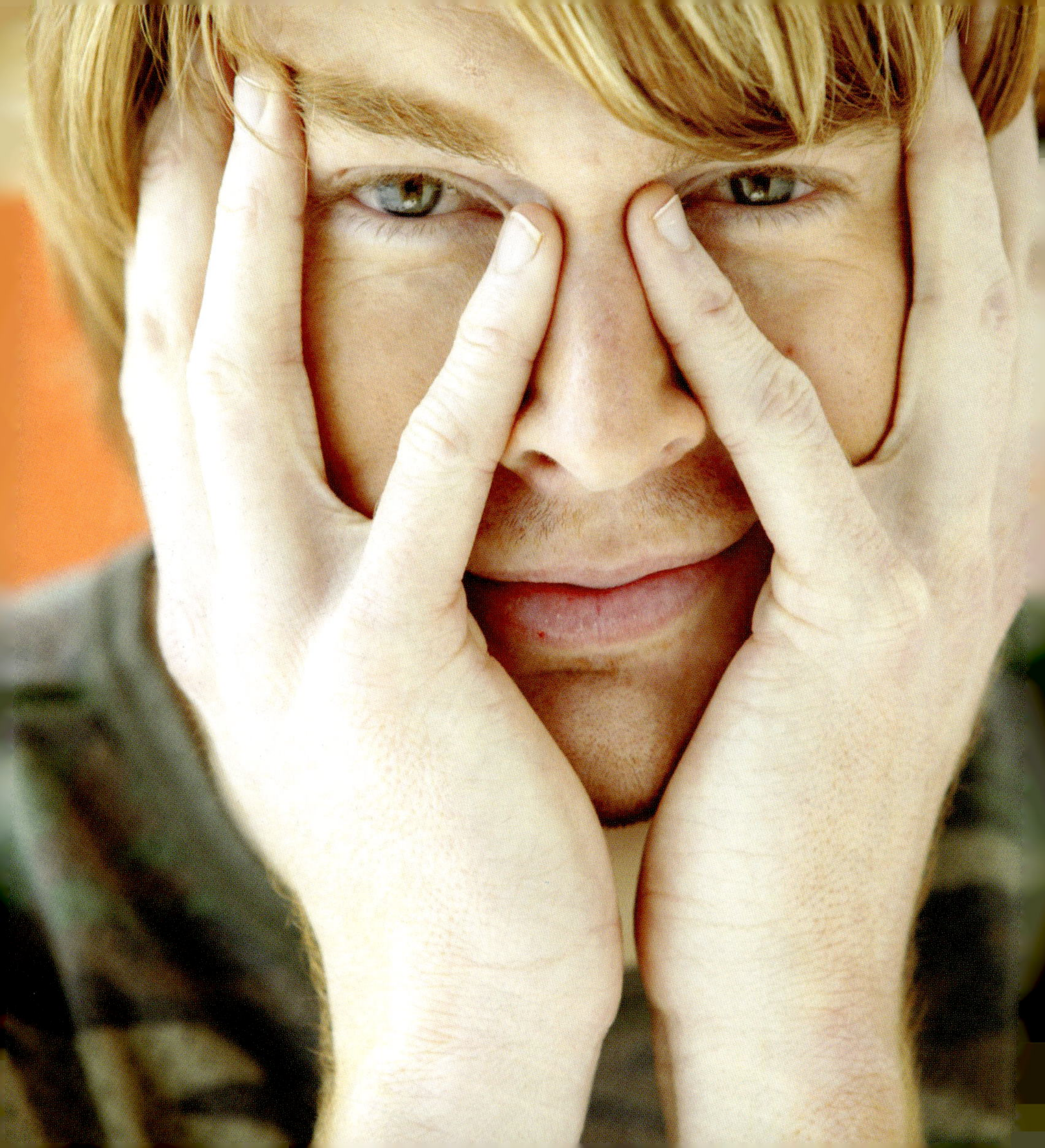

5.
WHEN PEOPLE TREAT YOU UNJUSTLY

You may be treated unfairly in life...

BUT GOD is a God of justice.

Jacob learned this firsthand when his father-in-law, Laban, deceived him.

"He [Laban] has cheated me [Jacob], changing my wages ten times. **BUT GOD** has not allowed him to do me any harm" (Gen. 31:7, NLT).

Laban tricked Jacob into working fourteen years so he would marry his two daughters. He defrauded Jacob over and over again, reducing Jacob's wages ten times (Gen. 31:41)! In fact, he tried cheating Jacob out of any wages at all (Gen. 31:42).

Maybe you have trouble at work with your wages. Maybe you have been deceived, defrauded, or denied your rightful due. Maybe you have been treated unjustly by those in power…**BUT GOD** has a way to fix it.

Our God is a God of justice. He promises that truth will eventually surface and right will be done.

You may be treated unfairly in life…**BUT GOD will work things out for those who trust in Him!**

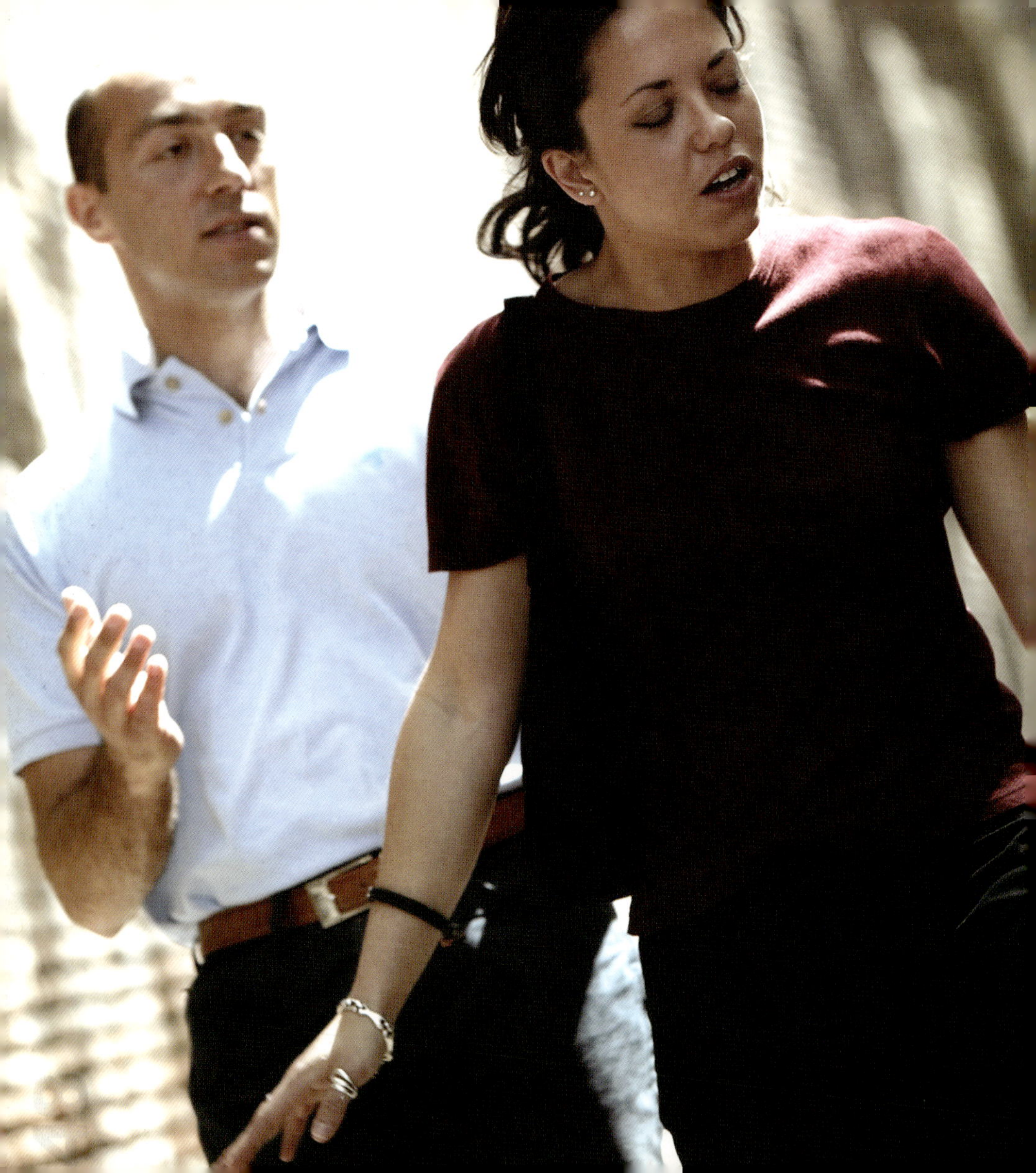

6.
WHEN FAMILY TURNS ON YOU

Even those close to us can turn against us… BUT GOD delivers us from their plans.

Just think of Joseph and the cruelty he had to put up with from his brothers.

"These patriarchs were jealous of their brother Joseph, and they sold him to be a slave in Egypt. **BUT GOD** was with him and rescued him from all his troubles" (Acts 7:9–10, NLT).

Joseph was his father's favorite son—which didn't go over too well with his brothers. To make matters worse, Joseph kept having dreams that he would one day be a great ruler—which included ruling over his family.

His brothers' jealousy and hatred grew and grew until they decided to kill him. When they couldn't take it anymore, they threw him down a pit and were about to leave him for dead—but then they saw slave traders approaching and decided to sell him instead.

Sometimes the worst things in life are actually part of God's incredible plan. All seemed lost when Joseph's brothers left him for dead and then sold him to the slave traders. But if it hadn't been for this, Joseph would never have gone to Egypt—and would never have become the great ruler God had promised him he'd be.

God delivered Joseph from the cruelty of his murderous brothers. And even more importantly, God used this betrayal for good in Joseph's life!

"And we know that God causes everything to work together for the good of those who love God" (Rom. 8:28, NLT).

You might think you've been forgotten, deserted, betrayed, and even left for dead…
BUT GOD will provide your victory!

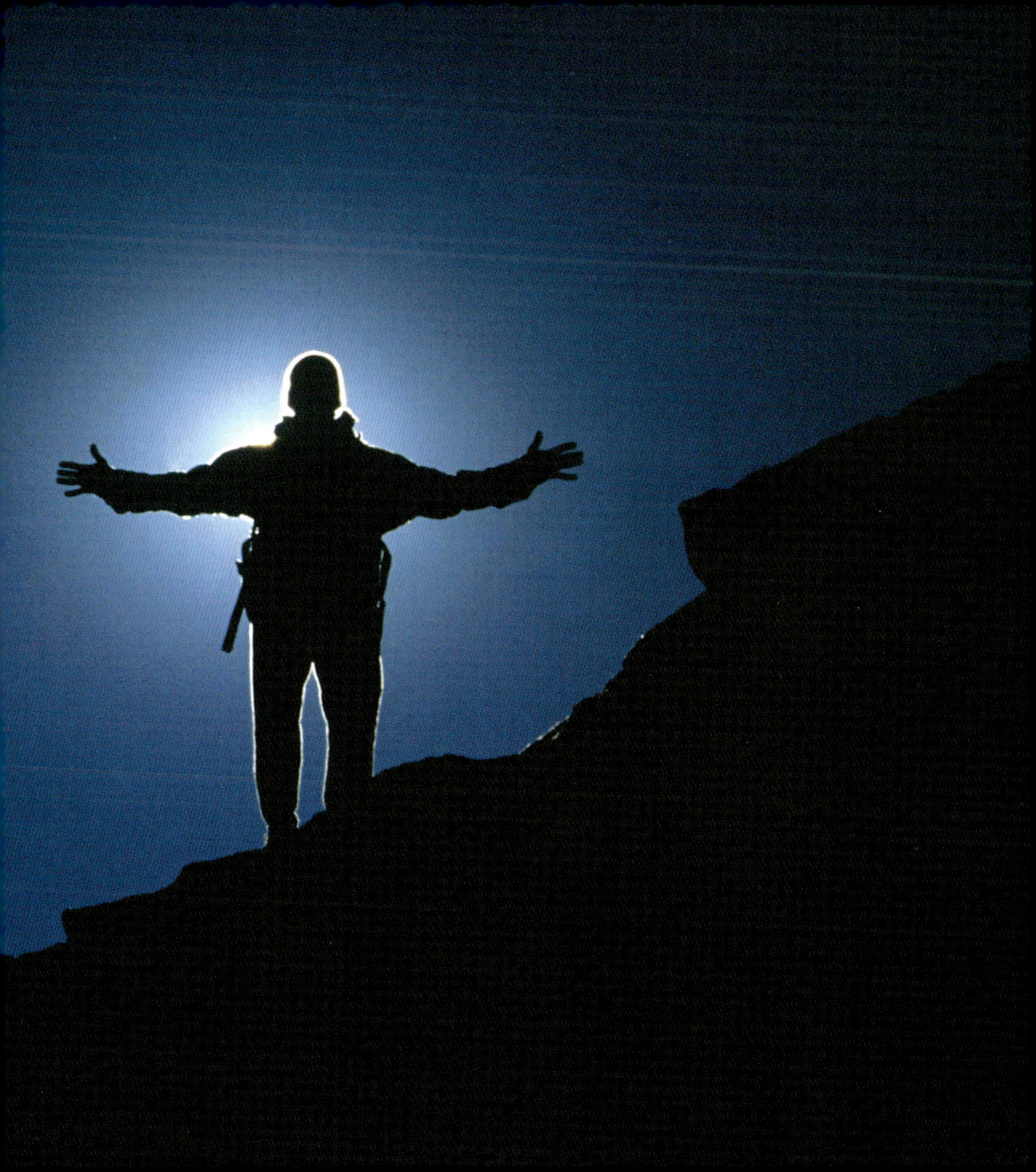

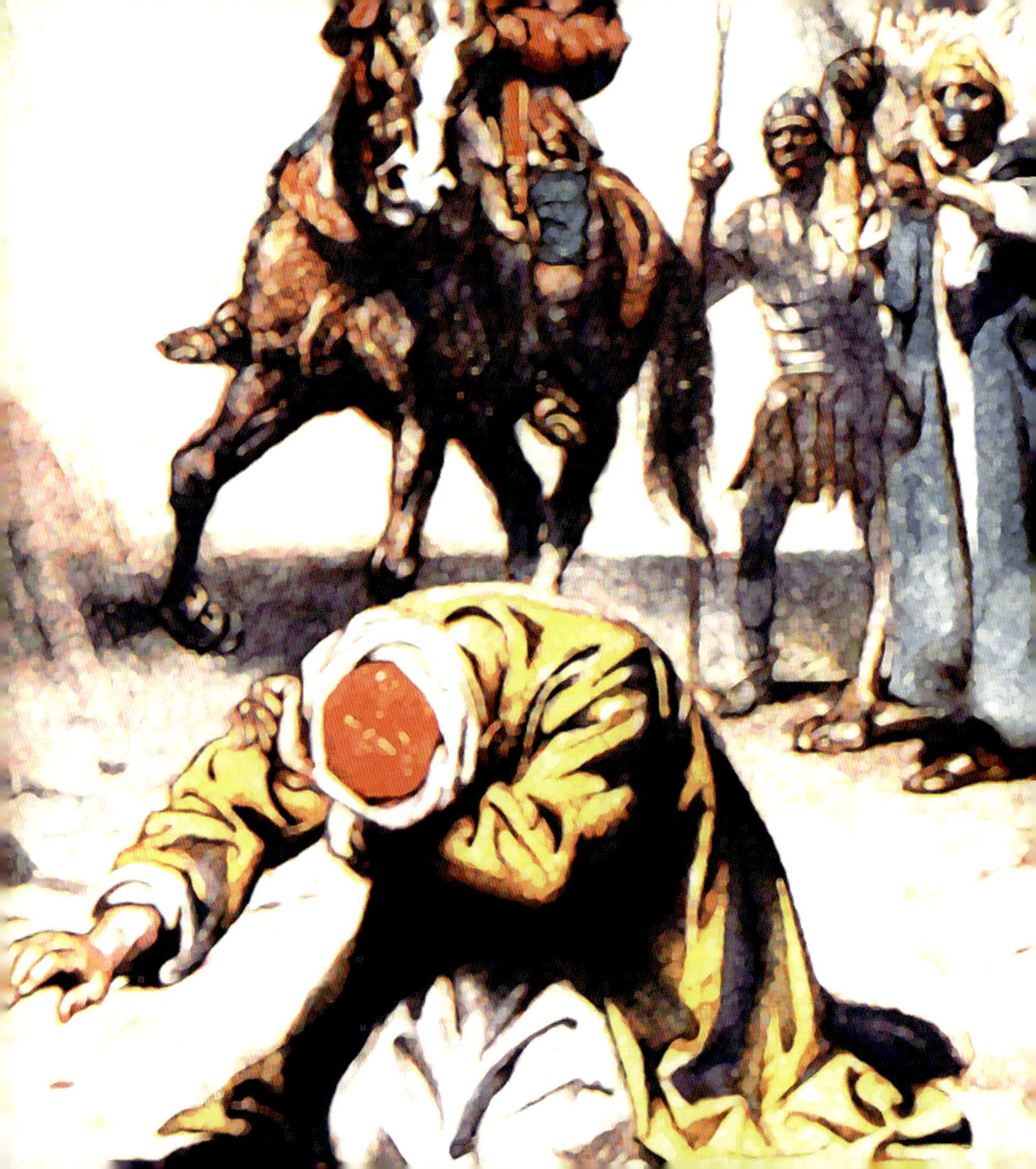

7
WHEN YOU'RE PERSECUTED FOR YOUR FAITH

People may turn on us when we stand for what we believe…BUT GOD protects us.

Think about Paul. Some of his own people turned against him when he began preaching Christ.

As he said in Acts 26:21–22, "Some Jews arrested me in the Temple for preaching this, and they tried to kill me. **BUT GOD** has protected me right up to this present time so I can testify to everyone, from the least to the greatest" (NLT).

At one time Paul had been their champion. He had been committed to their cause—but now they wanted him dead. When we stand for Christ, we will create some enemies, even from among those who once claimed to be our friends. They may even try to kill us or assassinate our character.

But when we stand for Christ, Christ will stand for us.

Paul was arrested by the local police and thrown into prison. We might not get thrown into prison, but there will be times when the situation seems hopeless and we are helpless. We might not know how we're going to get through it.

Part of the key to getting through is keeping a great attitude. Standing for Christ doesn't guarantee that we'll be treated well. In fact, we are guaranteed just the opposite. "And you will be hated by all for My name's sake" (Matt. 10:22).

But remember, persecution is a reason for joy, because we know the God factor will bring us victory.

"God blesses you when people mock and persecute you and lie about you…because you are my followers. Be happy about it! Be very glad! For a great reward awaits you in heaven" (Matt. 5:11–12, NLT).

We may be persecuted for our faith… BUT GOD will protect us and bring us victory!

58

59

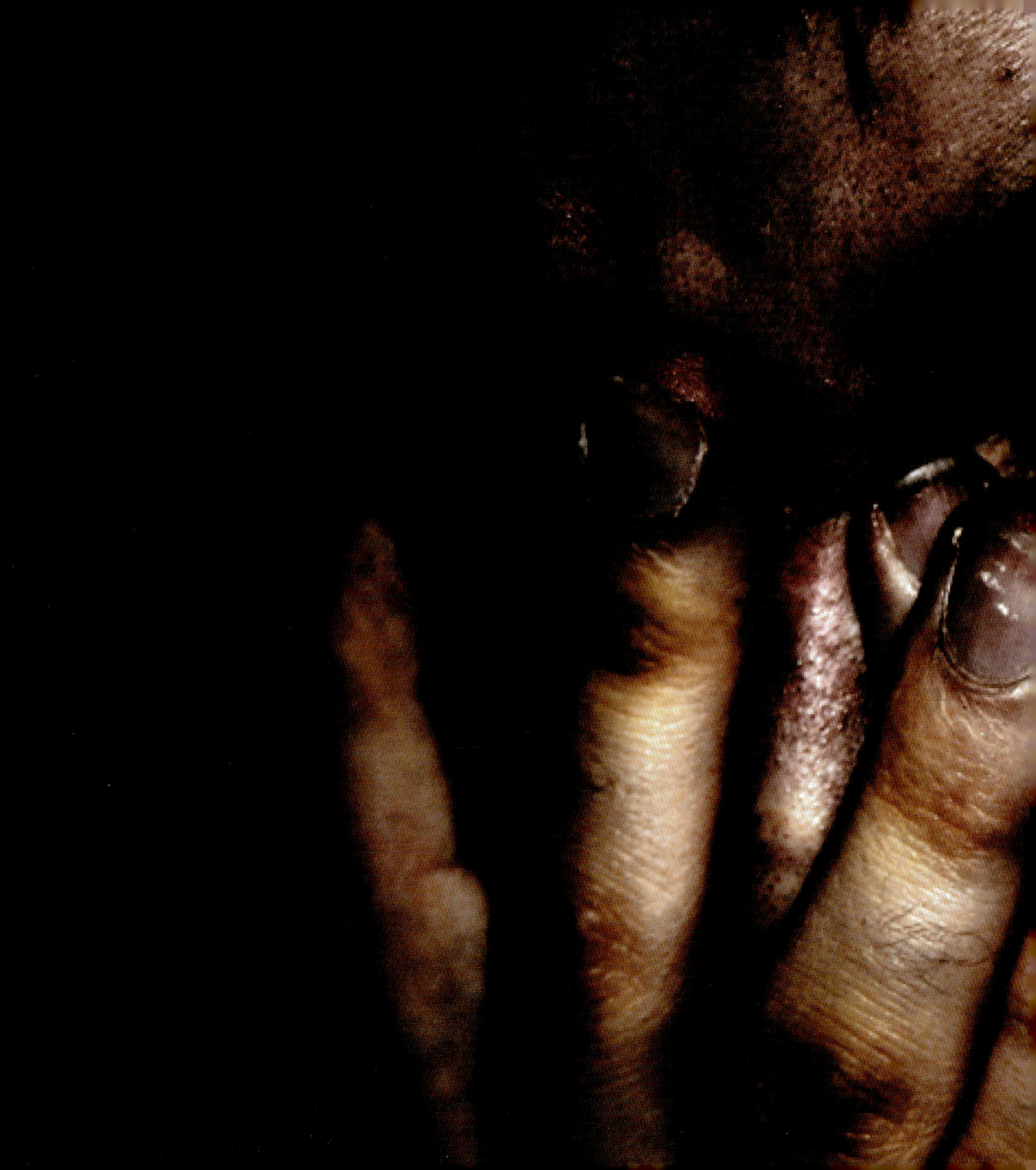

8.
WHEN YOU NEED GOD'S LOVE

We are undeserving, unworthy, and sinful…BUT GOD still loves us enough to die for us.

Romans 5:7–8 says, "Now, no one is likely to die for a good person, though someone might be willing to die for a person who is especially good. **BUT GOD** showed his great love for us by sending Christ to die for us while we were still sinners" (author's paraphrase).

All of us have done wrong at some time. "For all have sinned and fall short of the glory of God" (Rom. 3:23). But that doesn't have to be the end of our road.

Read the next verse. It says that we can be "justified freely by His grace through the redemption that is in Christ Jesus" (v. 24). A guilty conscience expects judgment, which is what we deserve.

BUT GOD has planned mercy for us which we receive when we repent. He prefers to give us mercy rather than judgment, and His mercy is everlasting.

The greatness of God's love is that He sent His only Son to die on our behalf before we had even considered repenting. In fact, He showed mercy to us while we were still hardhearted and sinful against Him.

Who is there in this world with love like that…**BUT GOD** alone!

We may feel guilty and fear that there is no hope…

BUT GOD shows mercy that sets us free!

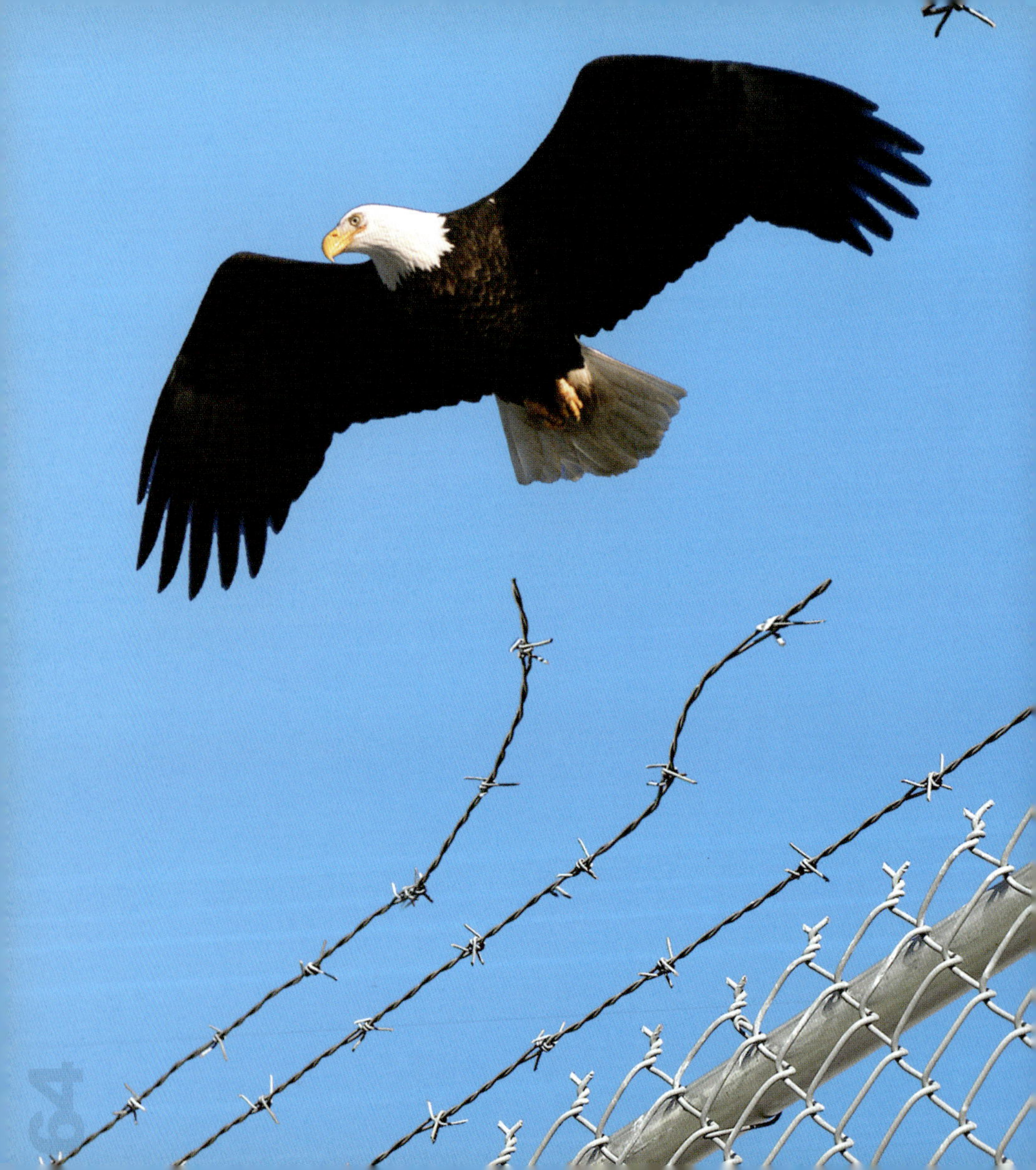

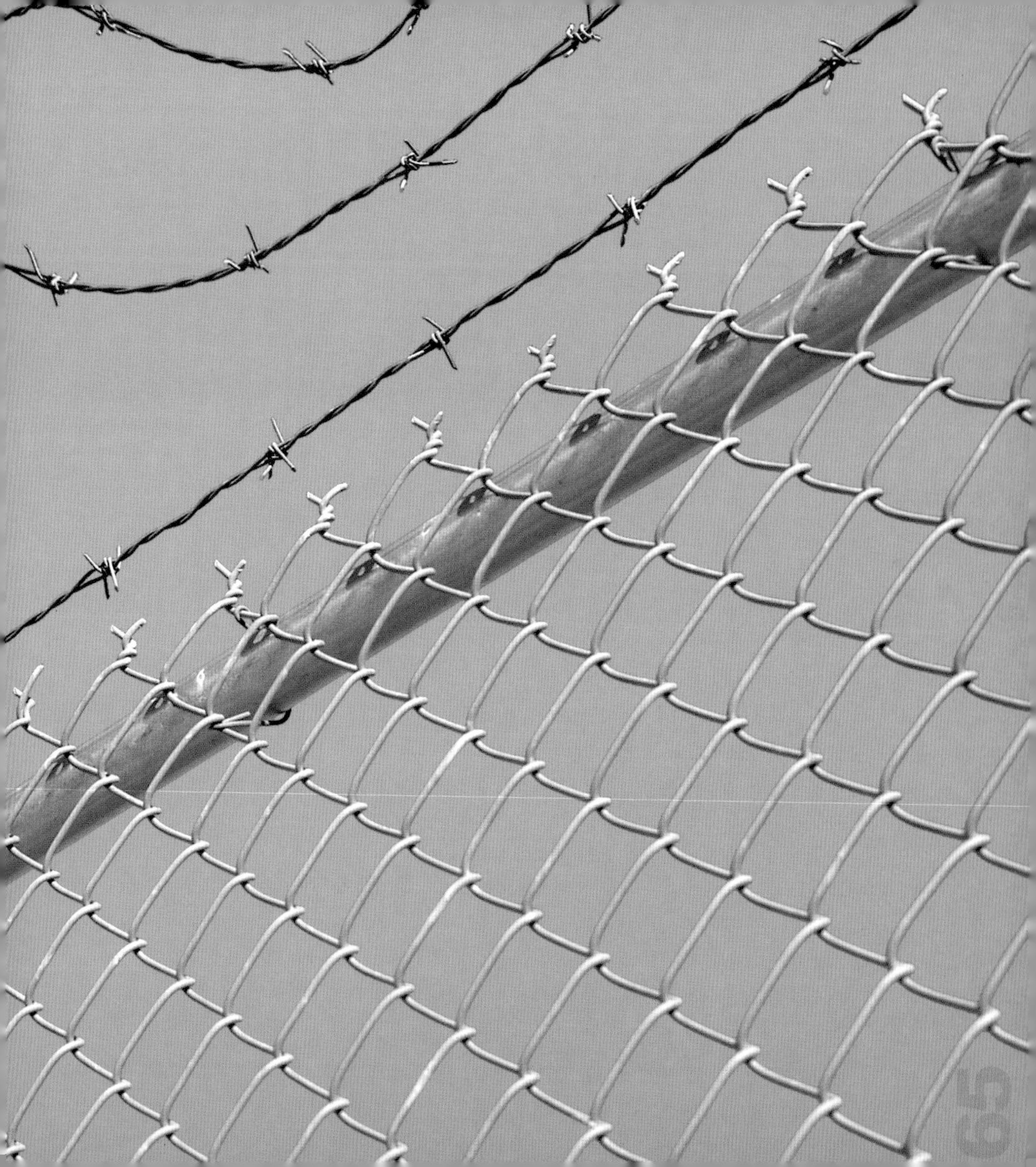

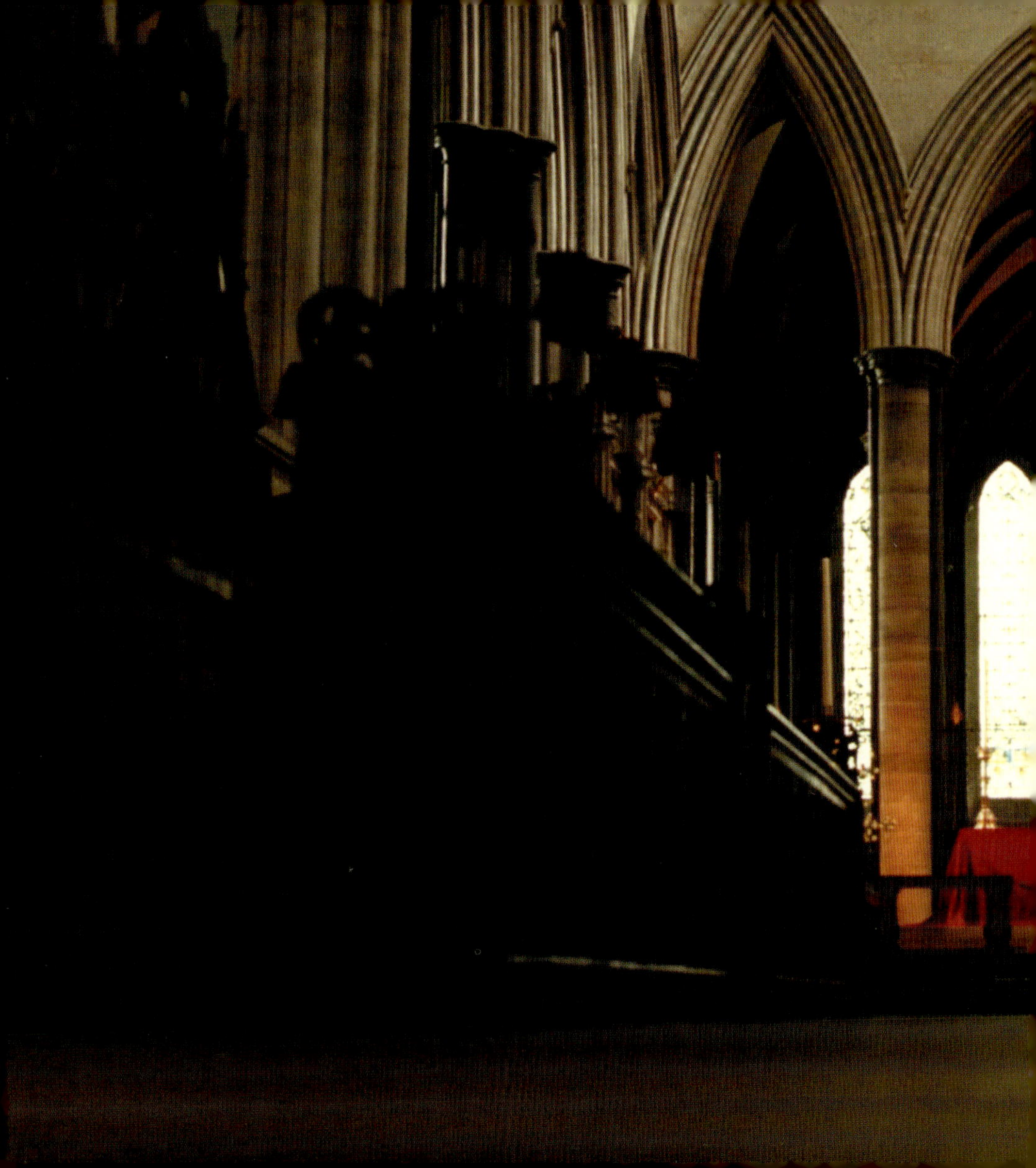

9.
WHEN RELIGION DOESN'T WORK

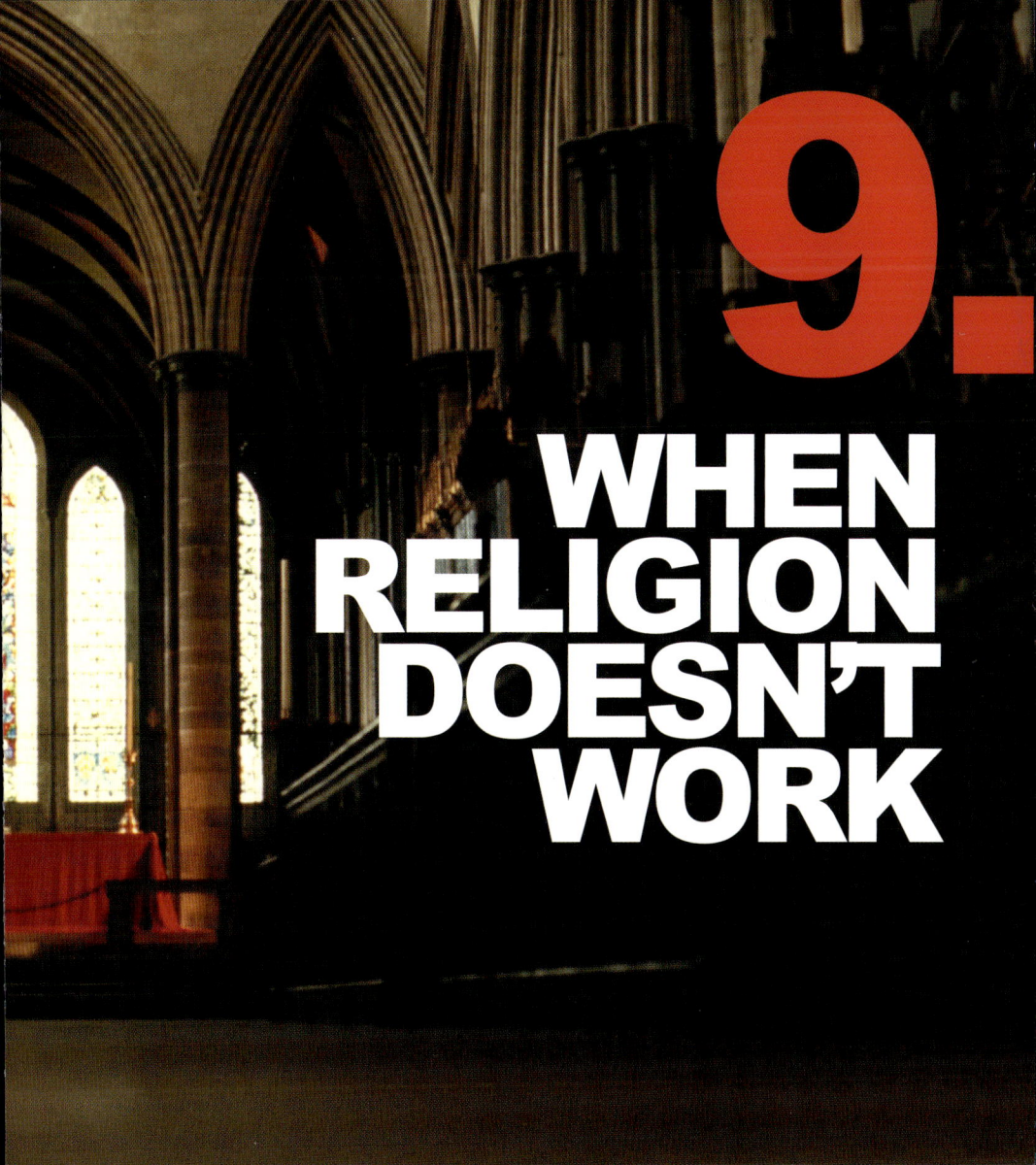

Religion and keeping the law cannot save us...**BUT GOD** devised another better plan.

Romans 8:3 explains, **"The law of Moses was unable to save us because of the weakness of our sinful nature. BUT GOD** put into effect a different plan to save us. He sent His own Son in a human body like ours, except that ours are sinful. God destroyed sin's control over us by giving His Son as a sacrifice for our sins" (author's paraphrase).

We want to be right with God, with ourselves, and with our life, yet our conscience rails against us every day. We try to do the right thing, but we consistently fall short of our expectations.

We need to give up things like smoking, lying, and hating. We want to start doing good things, like praying, loving, and helping others.

But it seems that all of our good intentions can be flattened by our own nature. It constantly beats us down.

BUT GOD has provided a way to overcome this problem. Christ breaks the power of sin. God doesn't just give us a

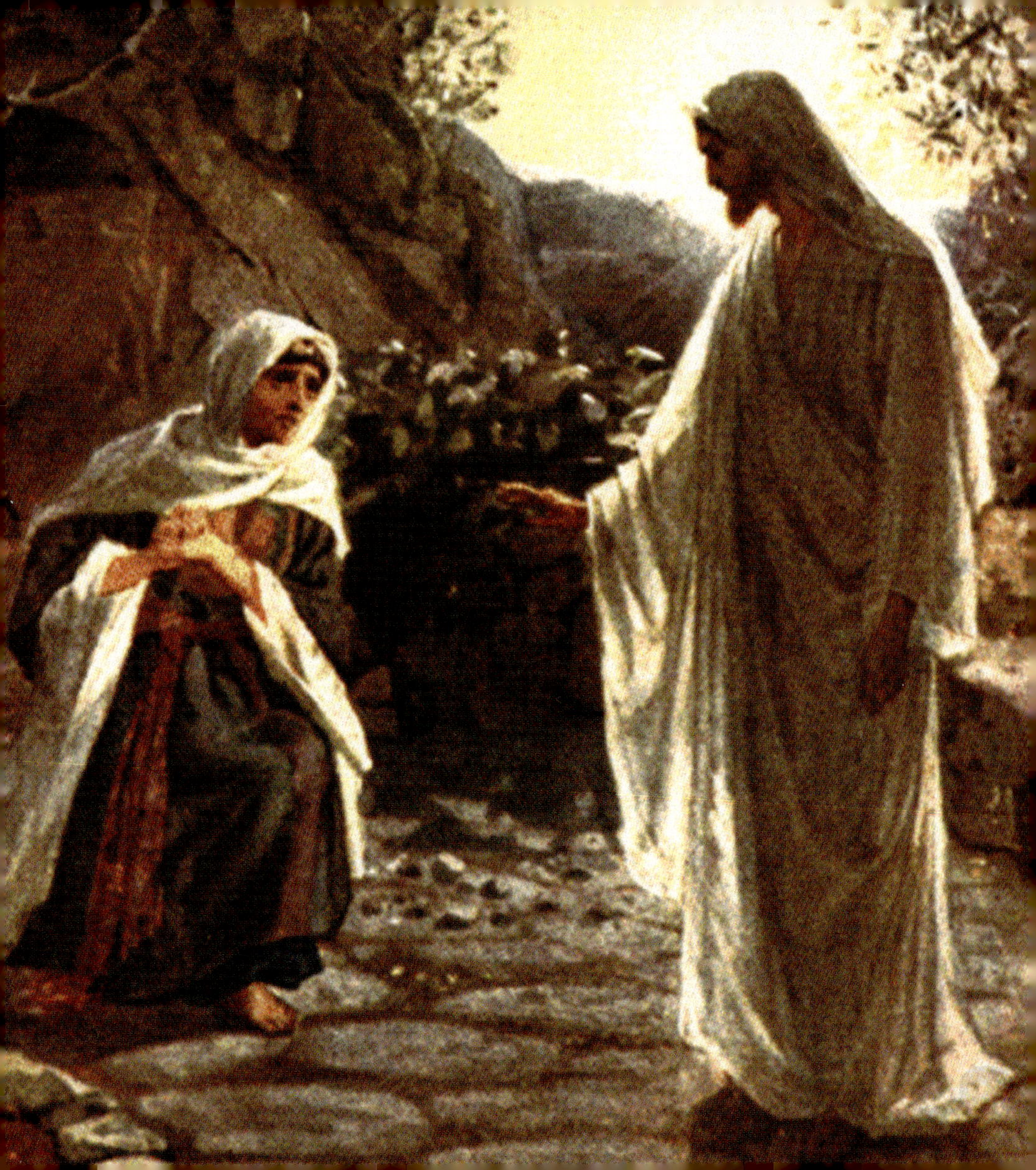

new set of laws to keep; instead, He gives us Christ, who overcame temptation, the devil, and even death.

When we live by the same power of Christ, rather than by religious laws, we are empowered to live a right life. Being made right with God through receiving Christ is the basis for salvation.

Once we've accepted Christ's gift of salvation, we are empowered to live life right. That's when we need to start living a life that doesn't need constant saving from perpetual sins, but one that pleases God.

It's impossible to do this on our own. It can only be done as we live in Christ and in the power of His Holy Spirit. When we decide to live in Him, we will live right. Our lives will please God and attract the favor of heaven.

Religion might not work for us… BUT GOD has established a better way in Christ!

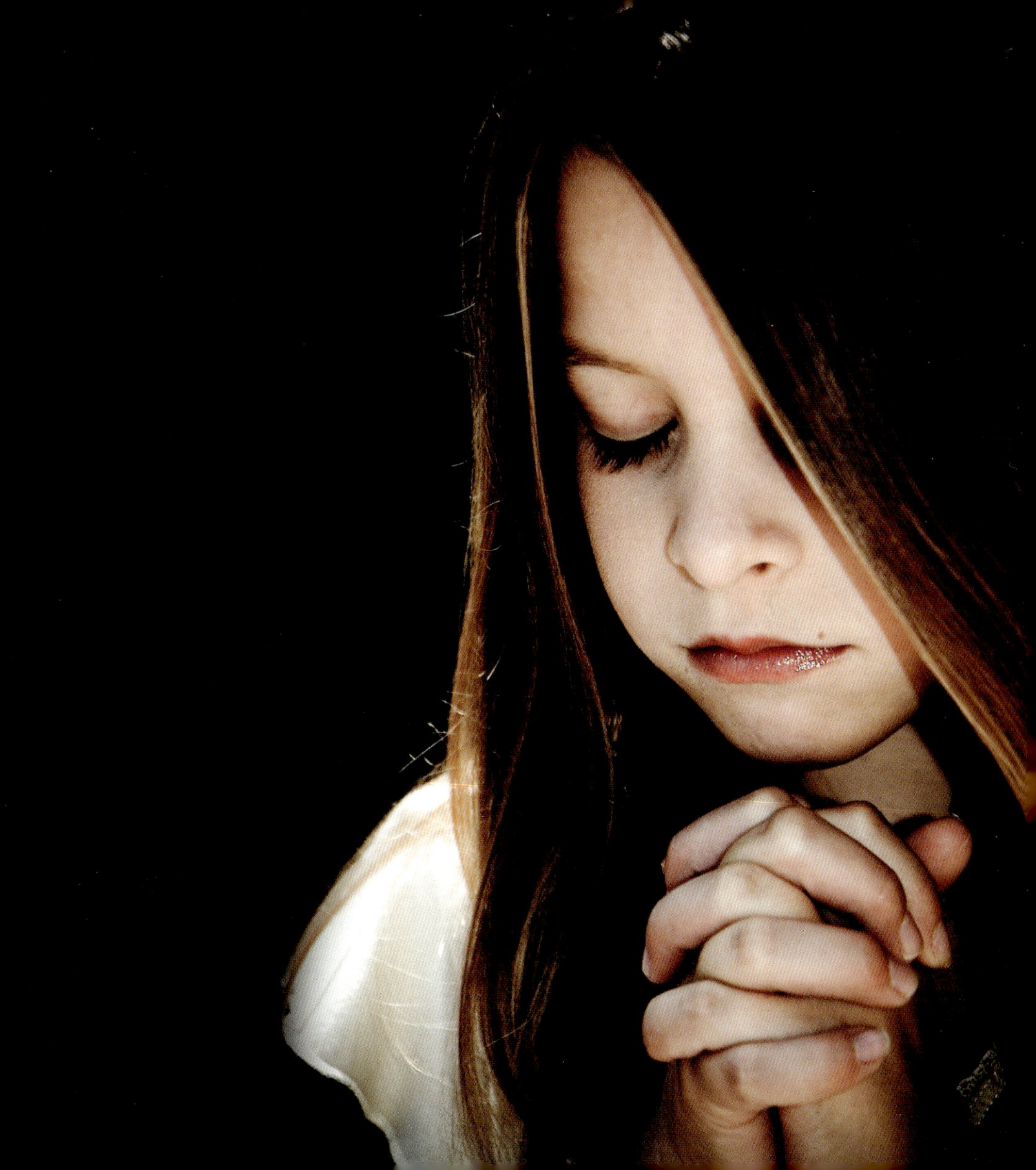

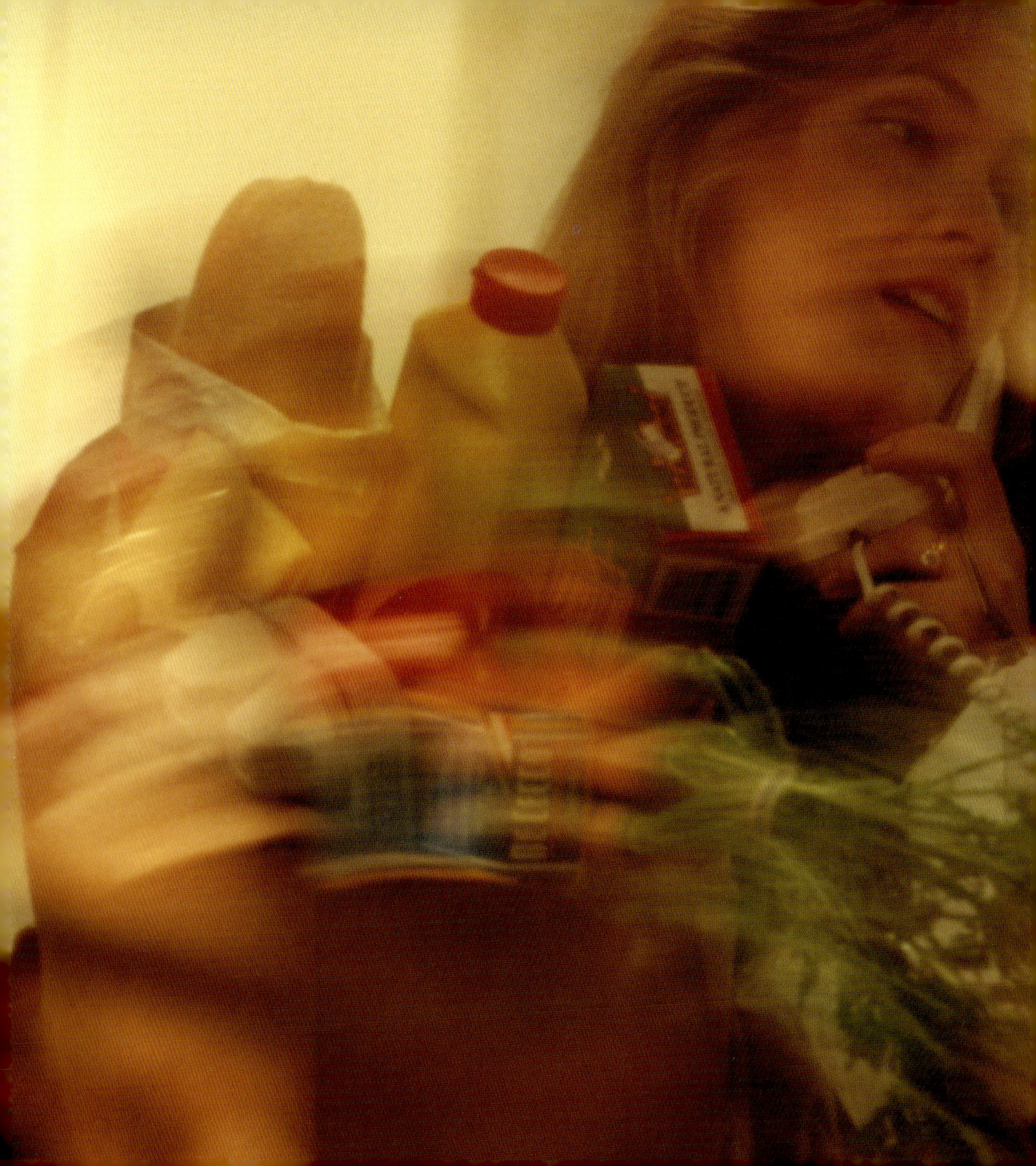

10.
WHEN YOU HAVE MORE PROBLEMS THAN YOU CAN HANDLE

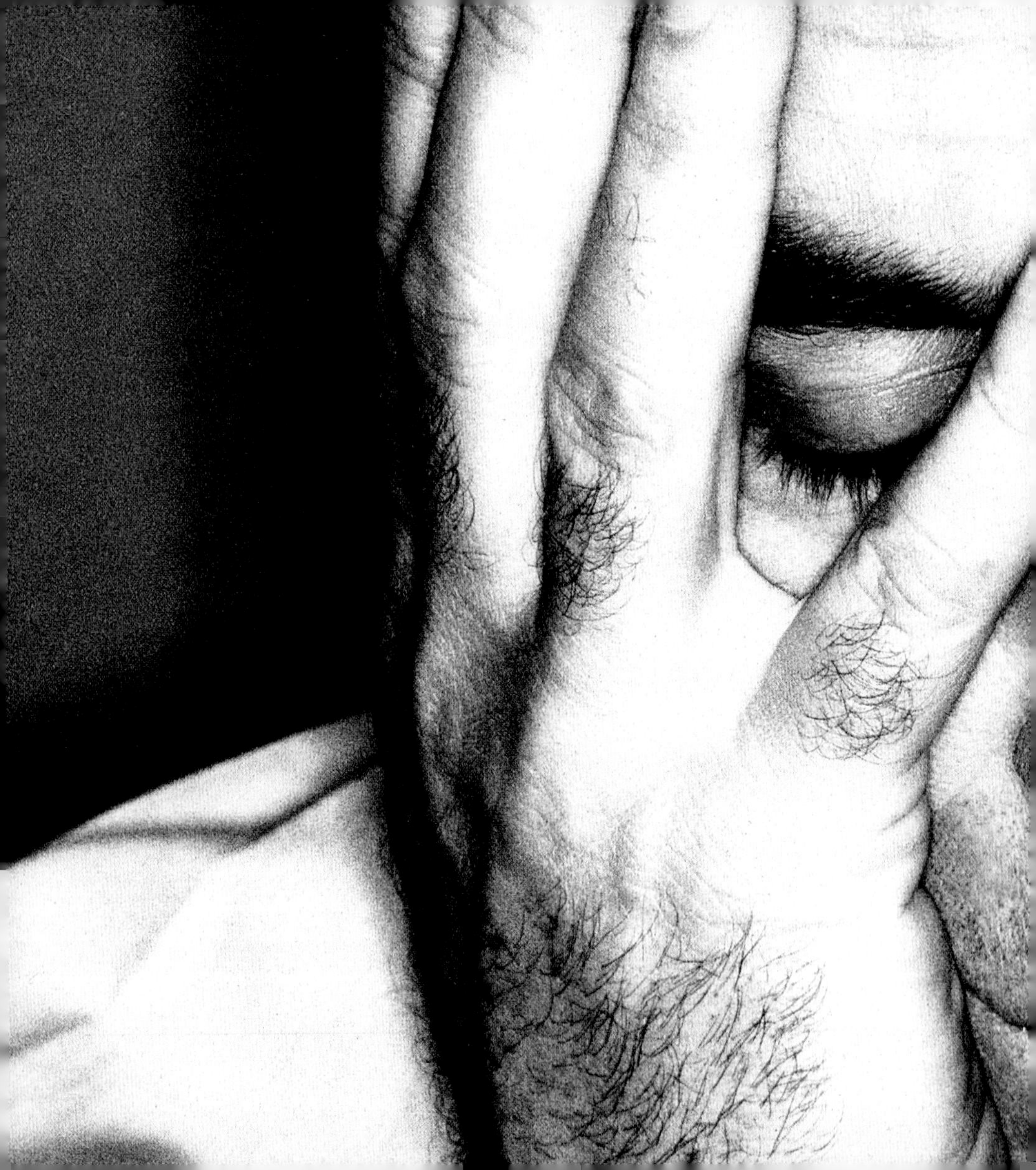

We might feel burdened by the worries of life…BUT GOD is in control and will comfort us.

Second Corinthians 4:8–9 reads, "We are pressed on every side by troubles, but we are not crushed. We are perplexed, but not driven to despair. We are hunted down, **but** never abandoned by God. We get knocked down, but we are not destroyed" (NLT).

Paul tells us here that he is pressed on every side by troubles. He has trouble from behind as his past keeps haunting him. He has troubles in front as people threaten him with repercussions if he attempts to accomplish his plans.

He is hindered again and again from going where he wants to go. Troubles come at him from the left and from the right. His friends desert him and criticize him, his strength fails, and things that should be simple become complicated and difficult. He says he is perplexed, (which means, "filled with uncertainty and difficulty").

Anxieties constantly barrage his mind. He worries about the churches he has started (2 Cor. 11:28). His enemies, the Judaizers, have written letters to some of his churches, claiming that they are letters from Paul and that he has changed his doctrine (2 Thess. 2:2). Many of the churches had been dragged back into legalism, some had become divided from within, and others had backslidden.

Through it all, though, Paul is trying to live above his own feelings of distress. He says, "We are hunted down." He has powerful enemies, who are constantly plotting and scheming to throw him into prison—or even worse.

He says there are times when

"we get knocked down."

What an understatement!

Paul was shipwrecked, stoned, imprisoned, whipped, beaten with rods, and left to die. Yet, in spite of all this, he continued to plant and build churches, write Scripture, and spread the gospel throughout the world—all because, as he declares, **"BUT GOD."**

No matter how many problems have congregated against you, flooding your world, seemingly drowning you, remember, **BUT GOD** will not abandon you. He will see you through to the other side. You can rise above them all.

"When you go through deep waters, I will be with you" (Isa. 43:2, NLT).

We may feel overwhelmed by problems…

BUT GOD is with us!

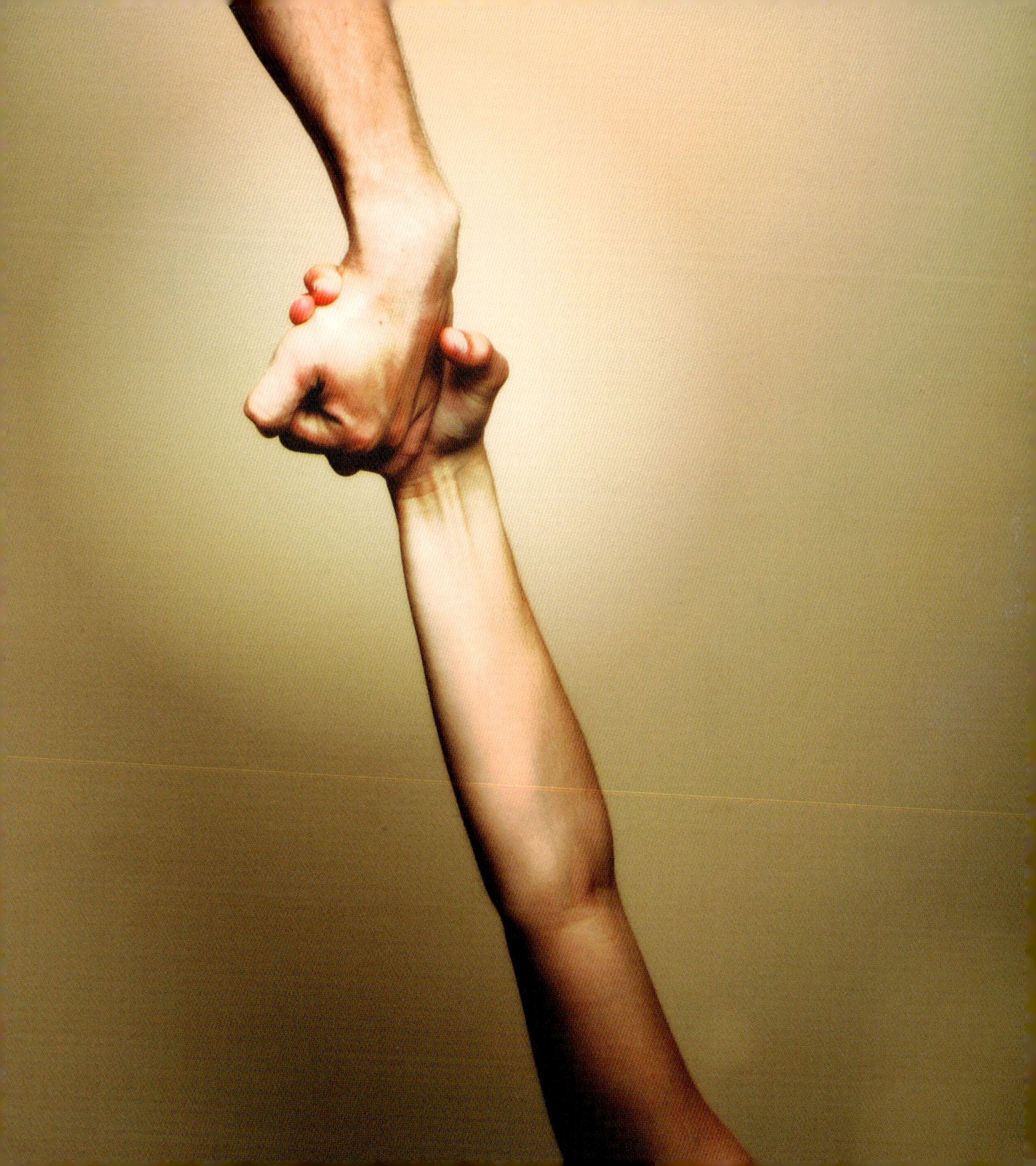

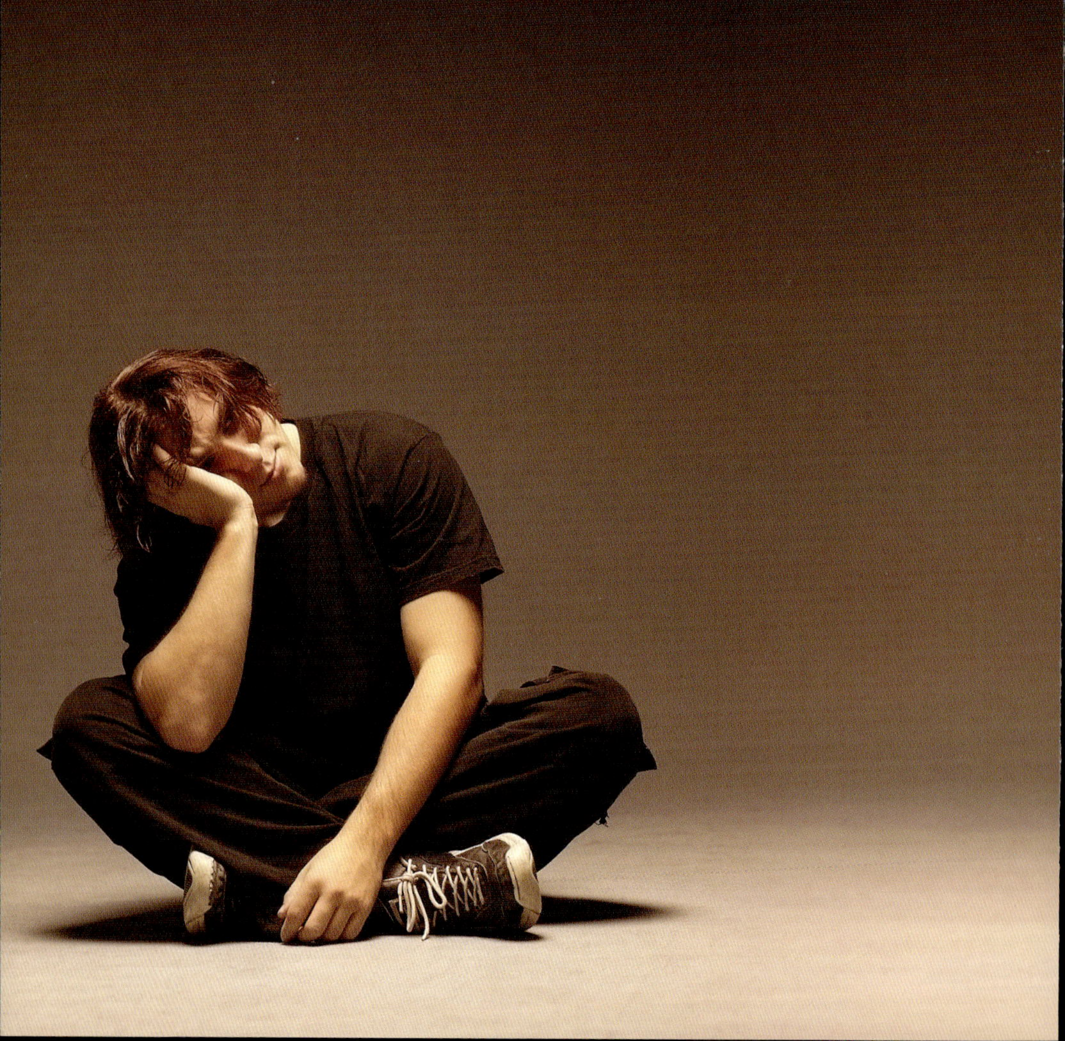

11. WHEN YOU'RE FEELING DISCOURAGED

We may sometimes feel discouraged...
BUT GOD puts courage into our hearts.

God reads our emotions. When He reads discouragement, He will arrange for other circumstances that encourage us.

Second Corinthians 7:5–6 says, "When we arrived in Macedonia there was no rest for us. We faced conflict from every direction, with battles on the outside and fear on the inside. **BUT GOD**, who encourages those who are discouraged, encouraged us by the arrival of Titus" (NLT).

In Macedonia, Paul had no rest. On the outside, he faced ferocious opposition; on the inside, he was worried. He had written a stinging letter to the Corinthian church, correcting them on a wide range of issues. He knew he had done the right thing, but he was worried about the impact the admonishment would have, feeling it may have greatly discouraged them.

BUT GOD arranged encouragement for Paul, sending his disciple Titus with a good report on how the Corinthian church had responded well to Paul's letter and had put things right.

We might feel distress about any number of things. We live in a high-stress world, and there is more anxiety and depression than ever before.

Even though modern society has experienced so many so-called advancements, none of these things can actually remove anxiety from us. Often, exactly the opposite is true. We can easily find ourselves with more stress in a high-tech world, rather than less. If we are looking to pills and technology to rid us of our worries, we will be disappointed!

Remember, you may feel discouraged and worried…**BUT GOD** is your courage and your comfort!

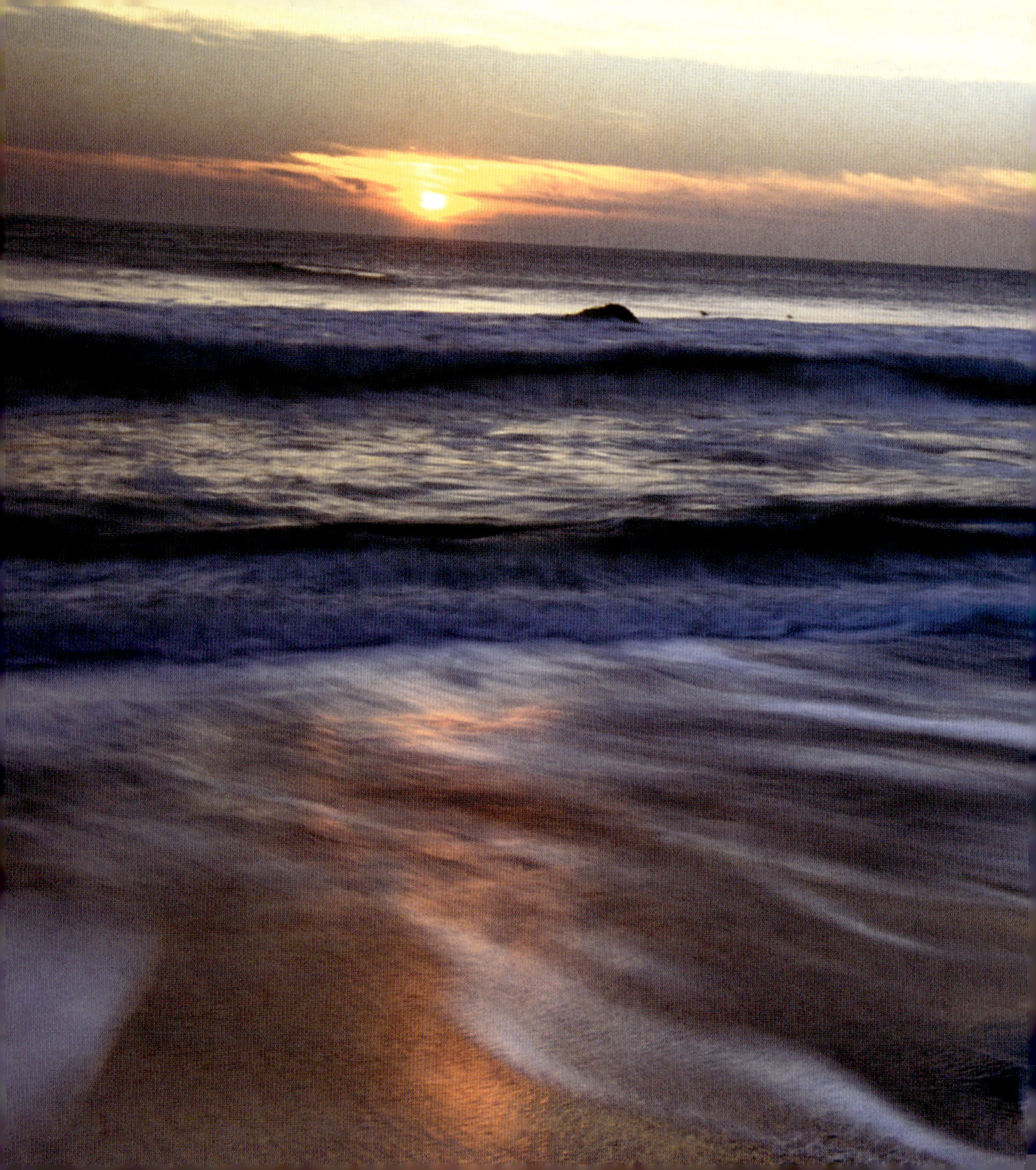

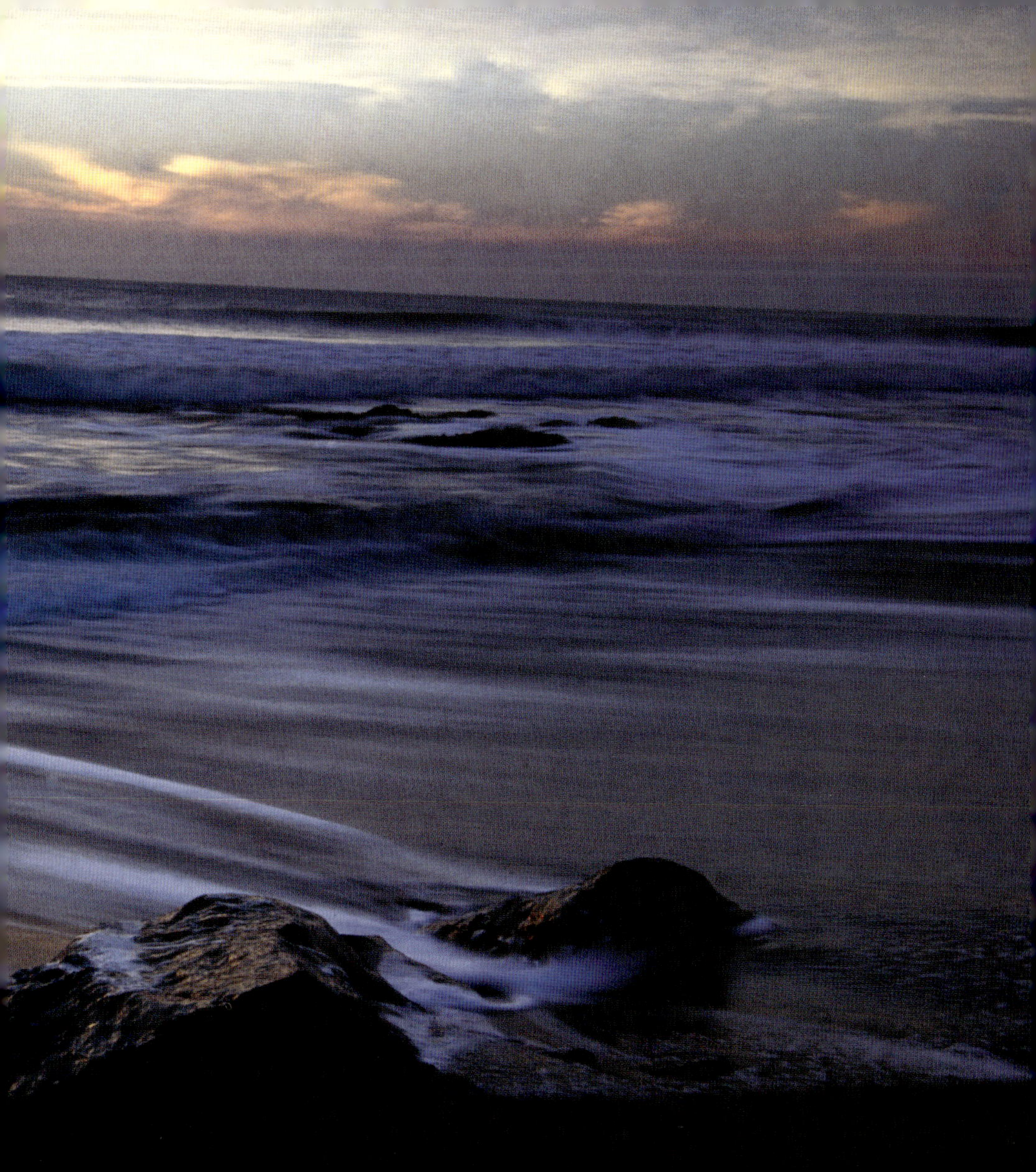

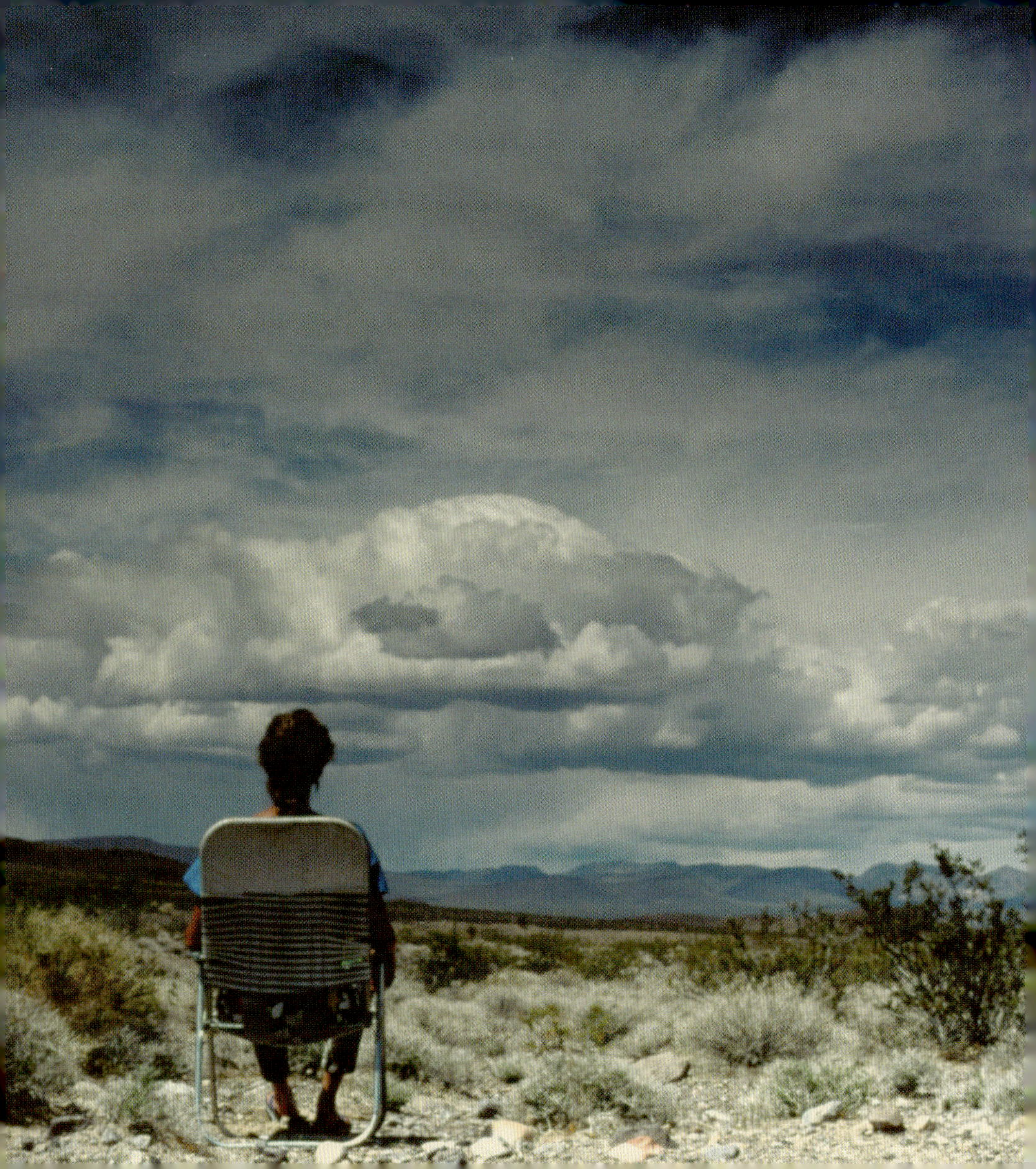

12. WHEN YOU FEEL DISTANT FROM GOD

We may feel far from God…
BUT GOD draws us to Him.

"By our very nature we were subject to God's anger, just like everyone else. **BUT GOD** is so rich in mercy, and he loved us so very much, that even though we were dead because of our sins, he gave us life when he raised Christ from the dead" (Eph. 2:3–5, NLT).

God is not one-dimensional. He is multidimensional. By this I mean that there are a variety of angles to the character of God. He can be angry with us when we are doing something wrong, yet still feel mercy toward us. This is the Trinity in action. This is mercy triumphing over judgment.

James 2:13 says, "Mercy triumphs over judgment."

Even though we can find ourselves far from God, He will not place Himself far from us. If we seek for Him with all our heart, we will find Him.

"And you will seek Me and find Me, when you search for Me with all your heart" (Jer. 29:13).

It's easy to feel that God is far off when we have done wrong. We can feel this because we think God is angry with us. **BUT GOD** is rich in mercy and willing to forgive us and draw us near to Him in spite of our shortcomings.

God revives us from a dead life.

He resurrects those parts of our life that have died. He can revive a marriage. He can resurrect our finances, our business, anything that has died and needs to live again. Jesus is the answer, no matter what the situation.

Everything may seem hopeless and we may feel far from God, **BUT GOD** draws us to Him!

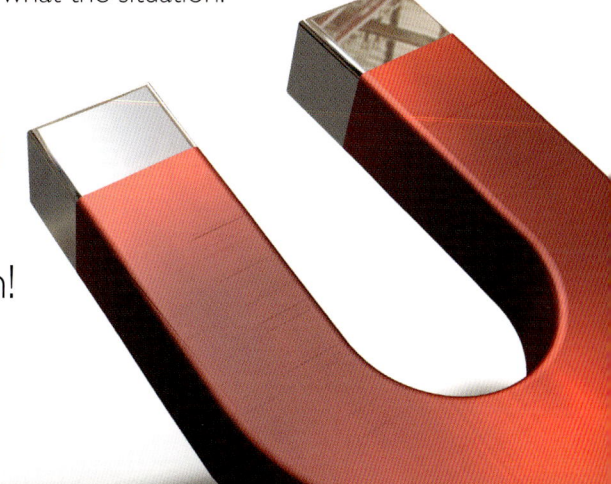

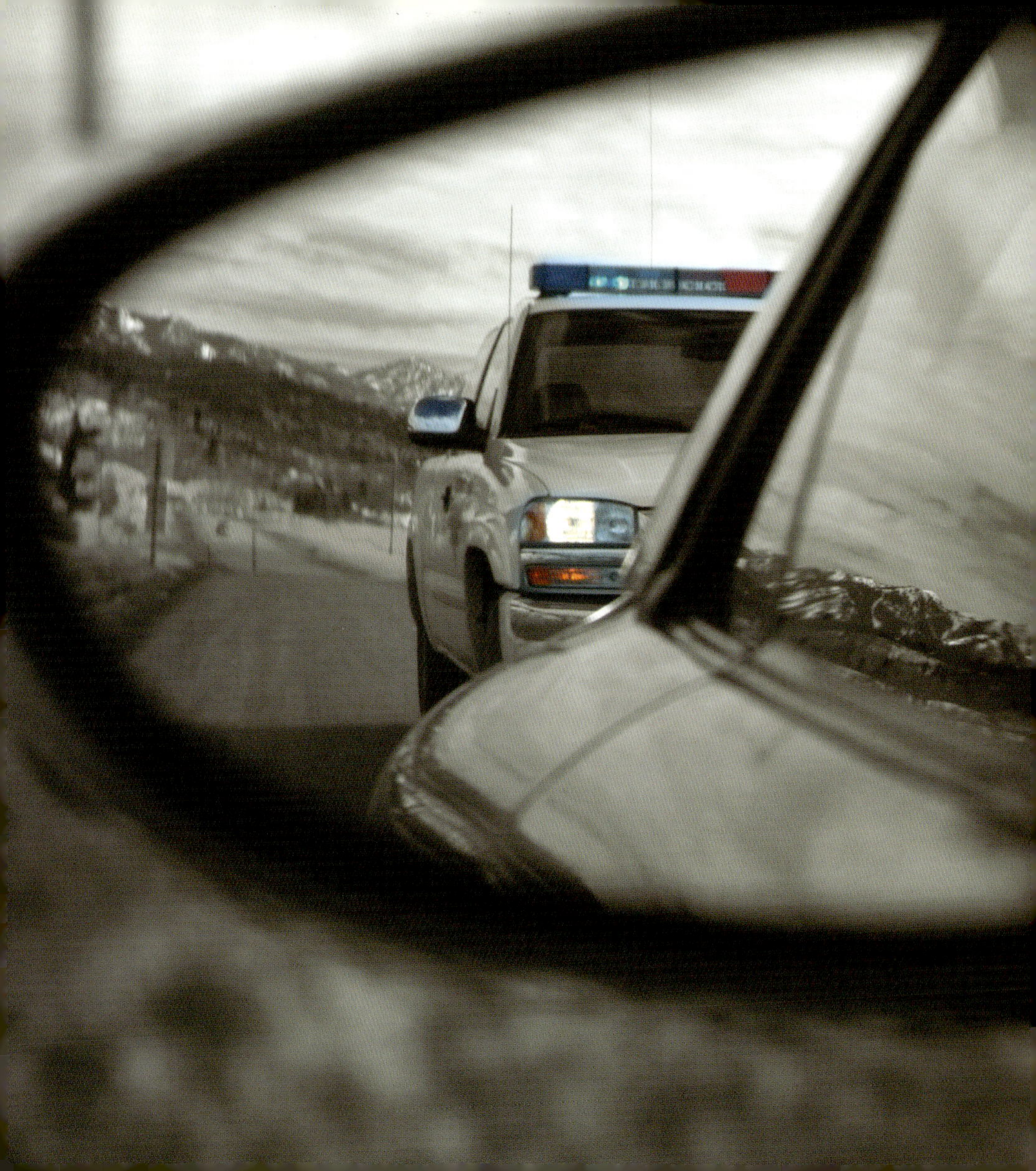

13. WHEN YOUR OWN MISTAKES THREATEN TO DESTROY YOU

We may feel trapped by death and sickness… BUT GOD can save us.

Psalm 49:15 emphasizes, "**BUT GOD** will redeem my soul from the power of the grave."

The grave tries to make its claim on us…

People try to bury us…

The devil tries to destroy us…

…BUT GOD is our Redeemer!

This means that even if I am the reason for my problem, even if I am the one who caused the mess, God can rescue me. He can make good of the bad I've done. As a Redeemer, He is able to take the worst circumstance in my life and make it good. No matter how bad things look, God can transform them.

Think about King David. He sinned horribly when he had sex with another man's wife, Bathsheba. Then she became pregnant; so, to cover it up, David had her husband killed on the battlefield. David then married her, almost as if he was trying to do the right thing by marrying a war widow!

But nothing was hidden from God, who knew David's sin, just as He knows ours. If we try to hide our sins, God will reveal them. But if we reveal our sins, God will cover us. That is the beauty of God's mercy.

Ultimately, judgment fell on David and he repented. God forgave him and pardoned his sins.

Bathsheba bore David a second child, named Solomon, who became the third king of Israel and was considered to be the wisest man in history. He was also the writer of some of the most sublime Scripture. **Bathsheba also became part of the genealogy that brought Christ into the world!**

We may mess up and create the worst disasters out of our life…

BUT GOD can fix it all and set us back on His straight path!

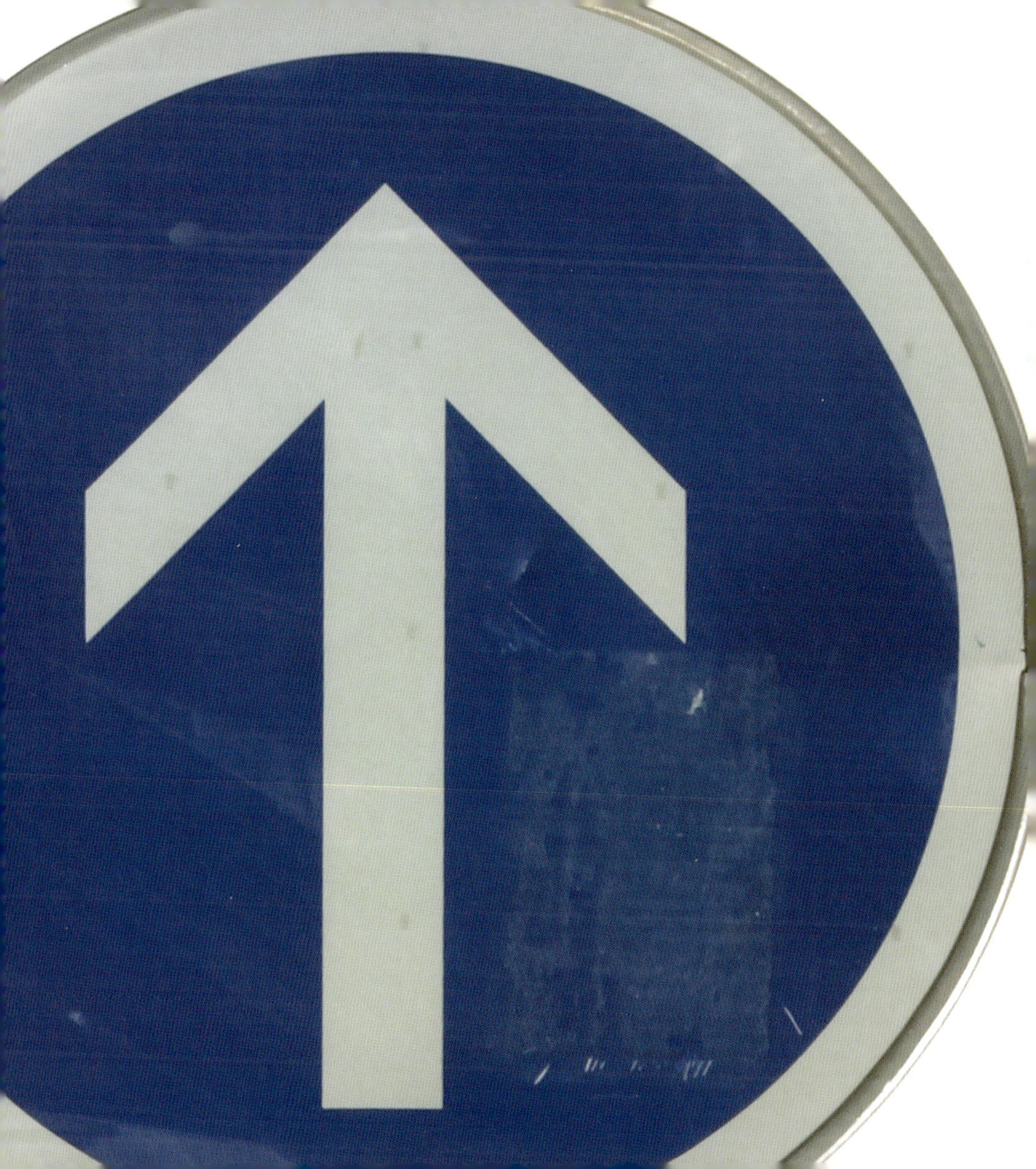

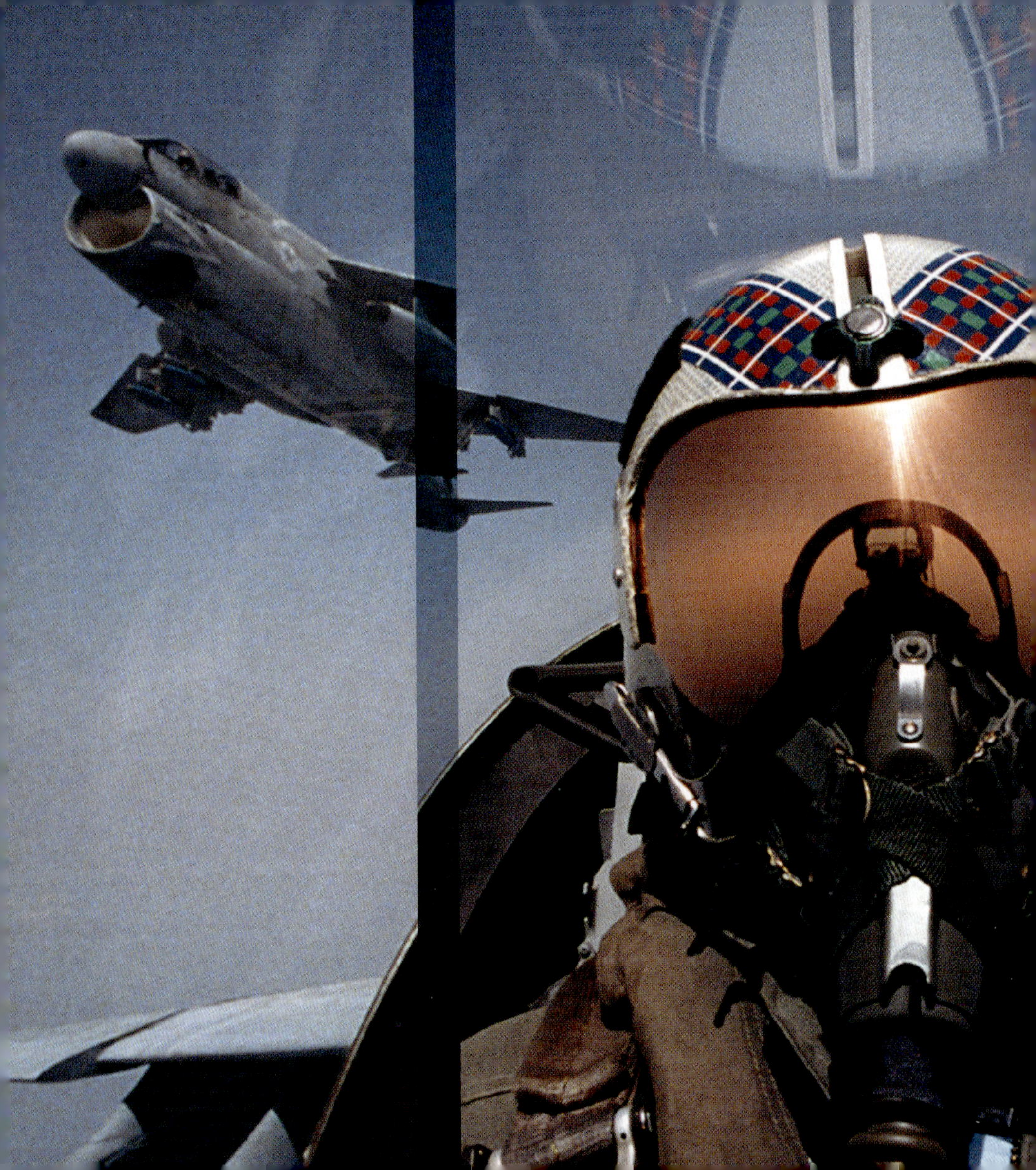

14.
WHEN YOU FACE ENORMOUS OPPOSITION

Large groups of people may oppose us… BUT GOD will ensure justice is served.

"The nations will rush like the rushing of many waters; **BUT GOD** will rebuke them and they will flee far away" (Isaiah 17:13).

There are times when the laws of our nation change to disadvantage us. There will be times when large numbers of people, maybe even entire groups of people, join together and rush against us.

When problems attack us suddenly, threatening to bury us, remember, **BUT GOD!** He will rebuke them, and no matter how many there are, they will disappear far away from sight.

During Israel's Six Day War, from June 5 to June 10, 1967, the tiny nation faced the superior armies, tanks, and guns of the Palestinians and several other Arab nations who were determined to wipe Israel off the modern map.

But that did not happen—God protected His people! In fact, there are accounts of barrels in the Egyptian tanks inexplicably melting, swarms of bees chasing enemy troops, and large, twenty-foot beings standing behind the Israeli soldiers, causing the enemy to flee from the battleground in terror.

You may fear the attack of an overwhelming enemy... BUT GOD will intervene and deliver the victory to you!

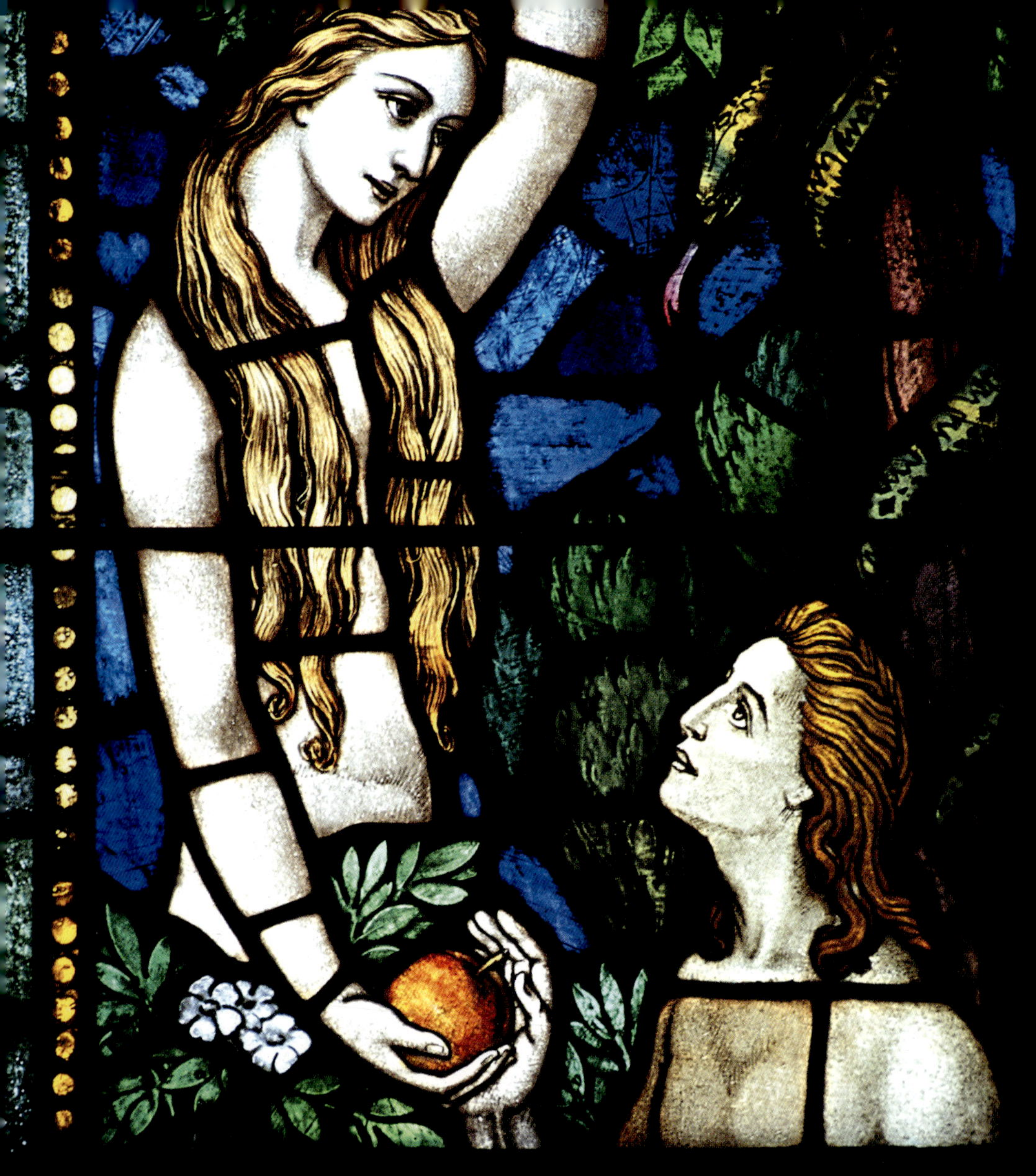

15.
WHEN TEMPTATION THREATENS

Temptation will try to destroy your life... BUT GOD will be your protection.

First Corinthians 10:13 says, "No temptation has overtaken you except such as is common to man; **BUT GOD**...will not allow you to be tempted beyond what you are able, but...will also make the way of escape."

The only person who falls in the face of temptation is the one failing to resist. The most powerful force available to us is our will, strengthened by the Holy Spirit. When we set our will against things that are overwhelming us, we will win the battle.

We may *think* the temptations we face are different and more powerful than those other people face.

We may *think* we are too weak to resist what is attacking us.

We may *think* we are powerless against the magnetism of temptation, drawing us in like a moth to a flame.

But we need to *know* that we are able to resist, because God will not allow us to be tempted beyond what we can bear. And God will always provide a way of escape.

Resisting temptation isn't easy, but with the Spirit's help, it can be done. Everyone is tempted; it is the human condition, something that's **"common to man."** The only reason we will fall is because we personally have not resisted the devil. Our will must be in line with the will of God resisting evil.

We will face seemingly insurmountable temptations…**BUT GOD** will be there to help us win the battle!

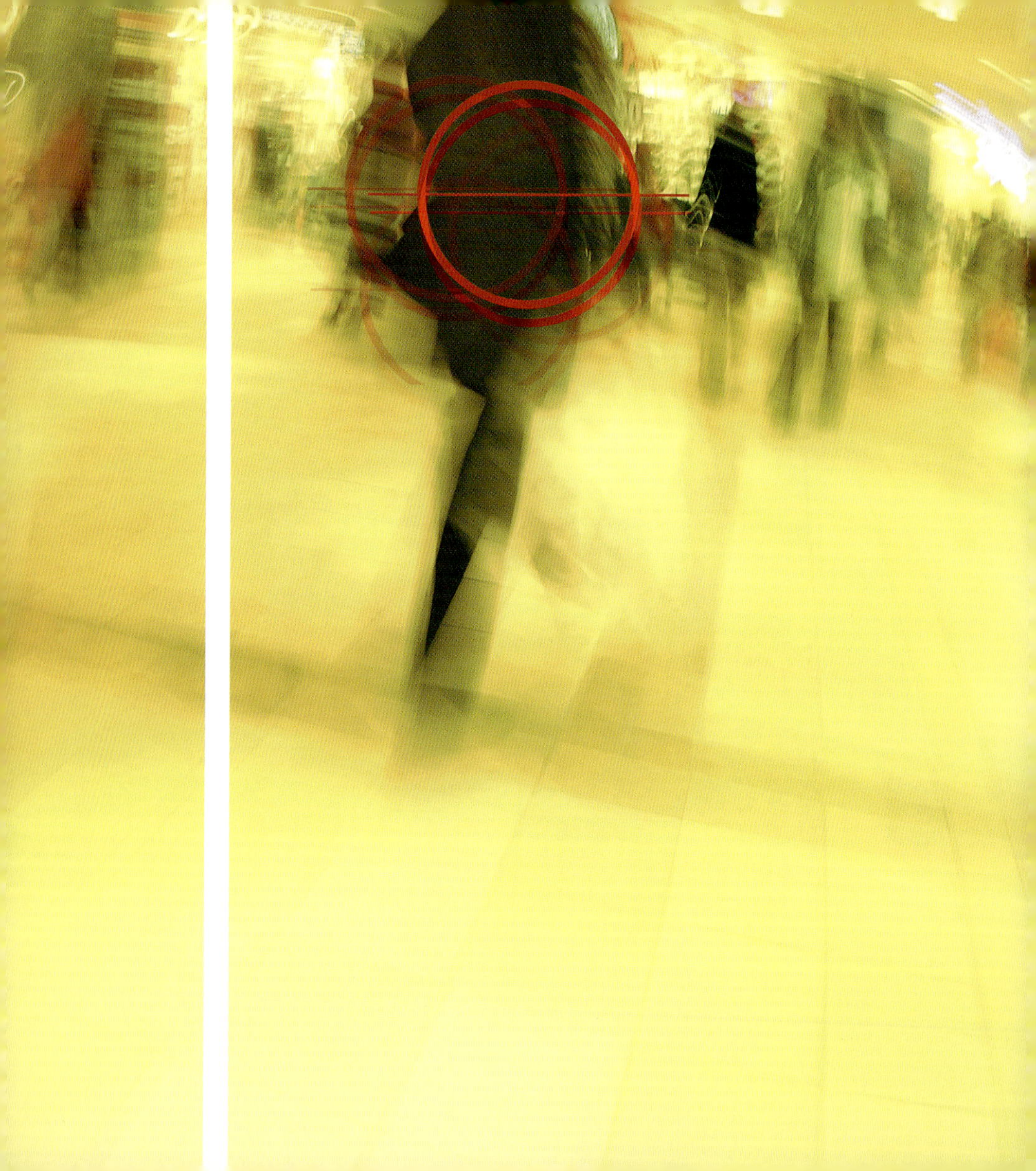

16. WHEN PEOPLE WANT TO GET RID OF YOU

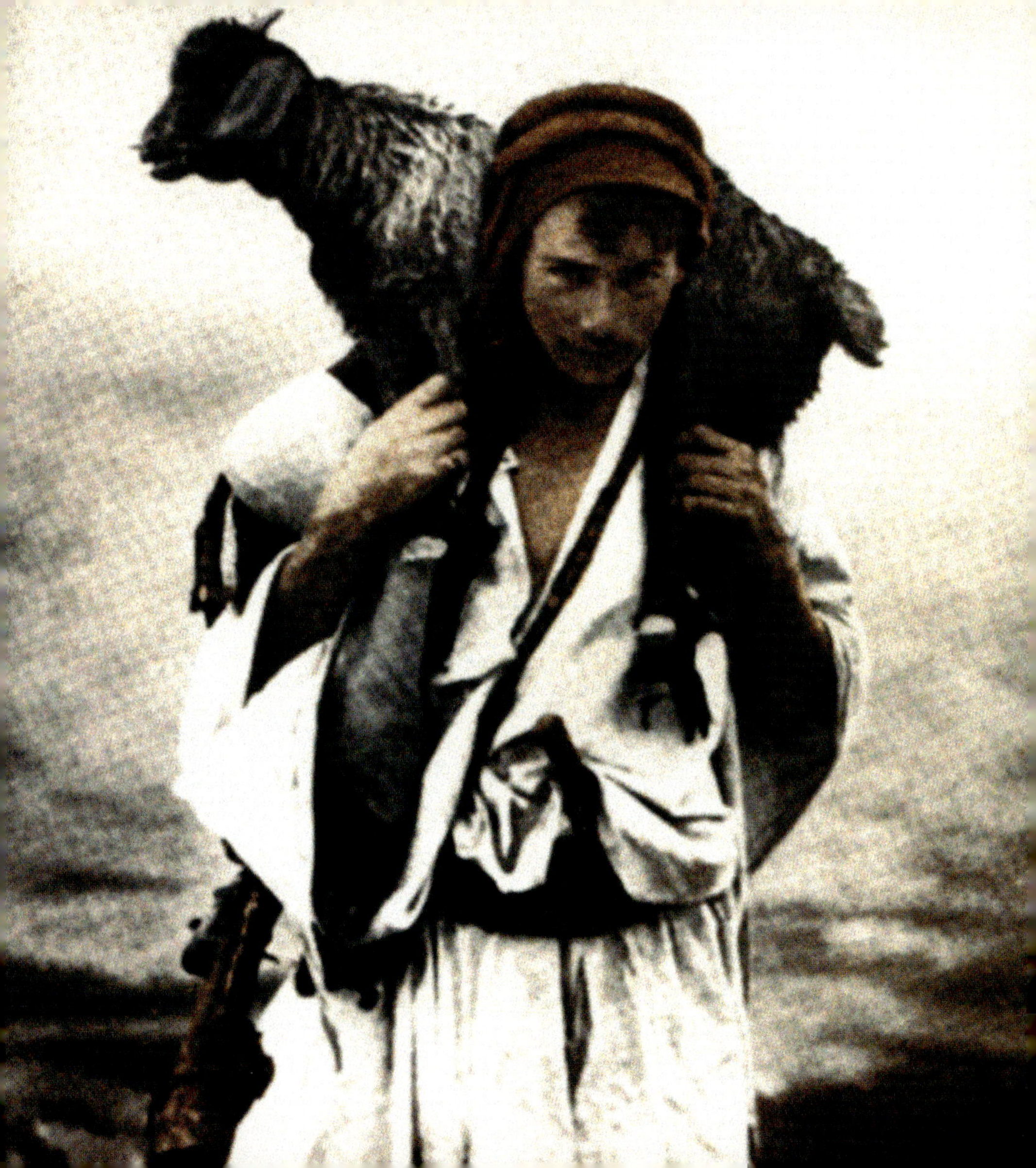

People may want to get rid of you...
BUT GOD protects His people.

Esther 7:9 records the words of the Israelite people: "'Look! The gallows, fifty cubits high, which Haman made for Mordecai, who spoke good on the king's behalf, is standing at the house of Haman.' Then the king said, 'Hang him on it!'"

In 436 B.C., there was an Amalekite man named Haman, who was prime minister to Ahasuerus, king of Persia. Haman plotted to exterminate the Jews…**BUT GOD** had other plans!

The Book of Esther tells the story of a young Jewish woman, providentially selected from hundreds of others to succeed the previous queen of Persia, who had disqualified herself by disobeying the king.

As queen, Esther uncovered a plot by Prime Minister Haman to exterminate all of the Jews. When Esther's uncle Mordecai refused to bow to Haman as everyone else did, Haman was infuriated and initiated a scheme to annihilate the entire Jewish race in Persia!

Haman did this by obtaining a royal decree from the king to carry out a massacre. He even erected gallows, on which he planned to hang Mordecai publicly on the fateful day when Jews throughout the land were to be slaughtered.

One night, however, the king was unable to sleep and began reading the historical records of the kingdom. He came across an account of how Mordecai had once prevented an assassination attempt on the king. The king ordered Haman to parade Mordecai through the streets in honor as a reward. Haman became infuriated and even more irrevocably bent on the violent destruction of Mordecai and all of his fellow Jews.

In desperation, Queen Esther called for a fast among the Jews and then approached the king, inviting him to dine with her. She also invited the wicked Haman, whose pride caused him to misread the entire event (he actually thought that he was the one being favored!).

The next day the queen revealed Haman's murderous plot to King Ahasuerus, who had just honored Mordecai for bravery—the very man Haman had set out to kill! The king was so perplexed as to what to do with his prime minister that he left the room.

Haman immediately threw himself at the mercy of Queen Esther, begging her to intercede on his behalf with the king, when suddenly the king returned to see Haman throwing himself at Queen Esther! Enraged, King Ahasuerus commanded that Haman be hanged on the very gallows Haman himself had erected for Mordecai—and the extermination of the Jews was shut down immediately.

There are large events and small details that God Himself oversees to ensure that all of His promises are fulfilled.

You may think that you are on the brink of destruction…BUT GOD will intercede!

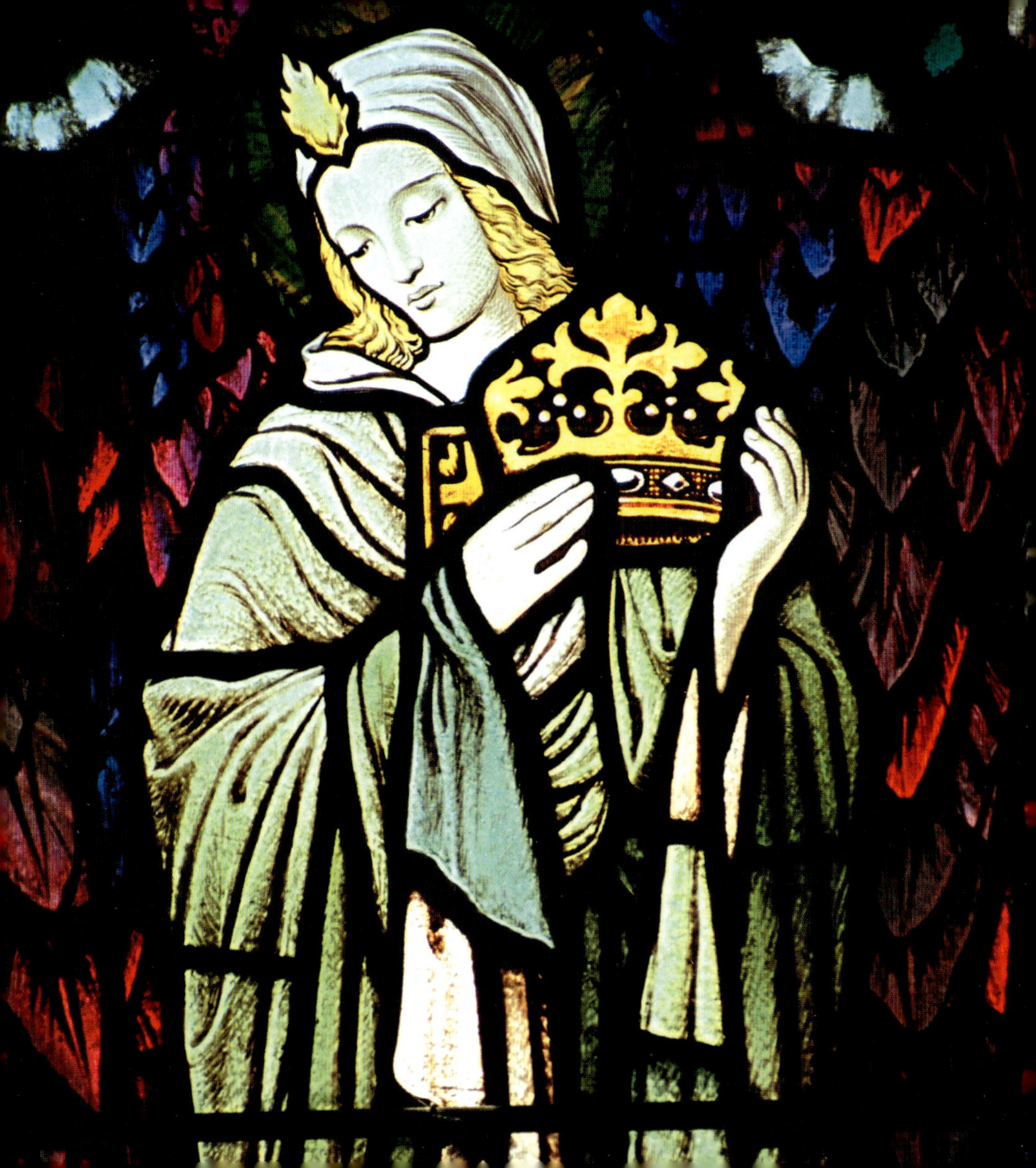

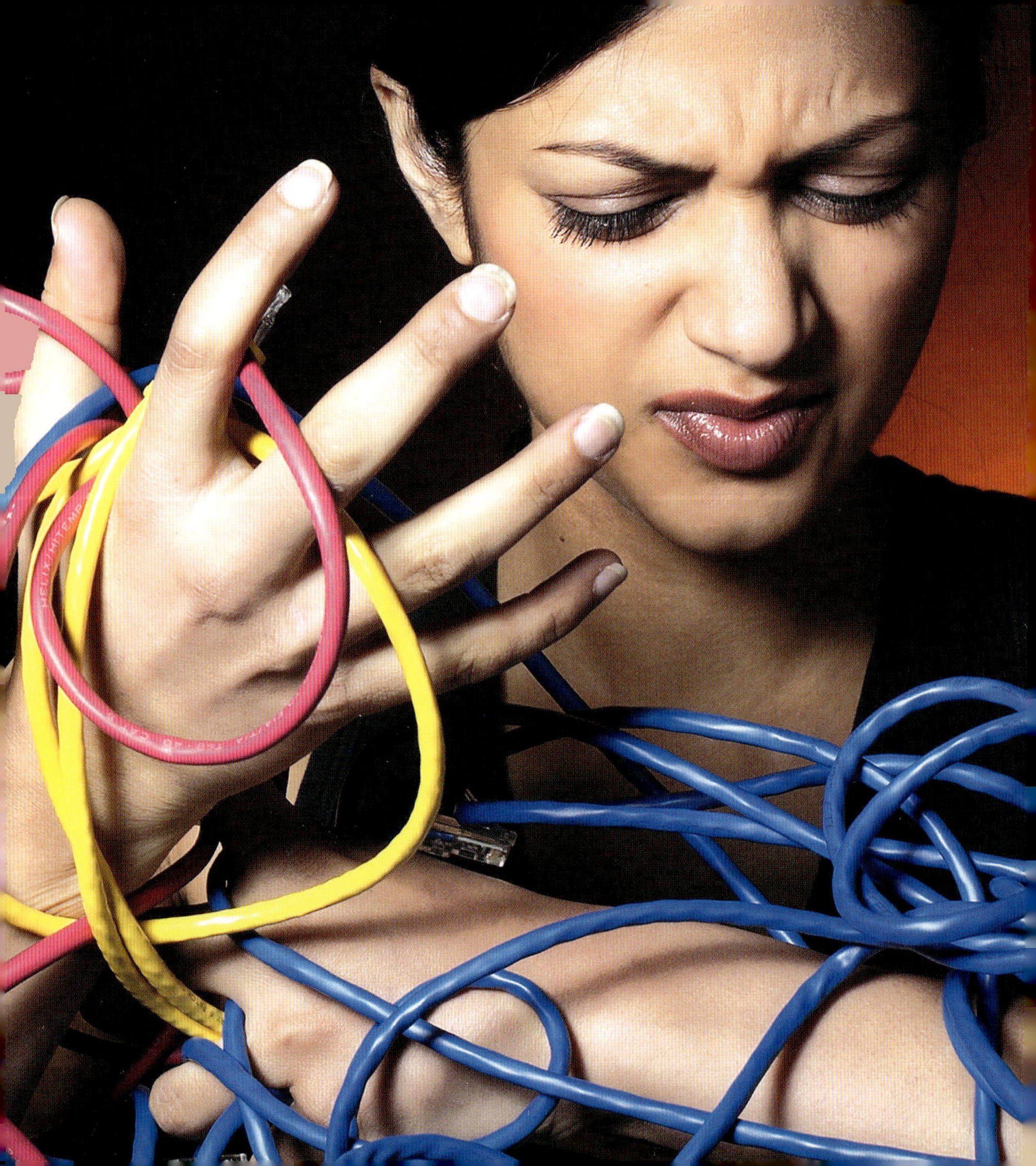

17. WHEN YOU GET YOURSELF INTO A MESS

You may make a mess out of life…
BUT GOD can fix it.

"**BUT THE LORD** provided a great fish to swallow Jonah, and Jonah was inside the fish three days and three nights" (Jon. 1:17, NIV).

The Book of Jonah tells about the prophet Jonah, who made a terrible mistake. He rejected what God wanted him to do and disobeyed God. Eventually Jonah was thrown into the ocean during a storm…**BUT GOD** protected him.

Jonah was called to be a servant of God, but he was unwilling to carry out God's command of preaching and prophesying to the people of Ninevah. Jonah knew that if he took God's message to Ninevah, the Assyrian capital, the people there would repent and God would show mercy on them. But Jonah was fiercely patriotic to his own Jewish nation, which had been attacked, plundered, and oppressed by those very same Assyrians, who were notorious for their cruelty to Israel.

Jonah wanted no part of the assignment, and he tried to run from God! He bought a ticket on a boat bound for a city called Tarshish, but a fierce storm arose and Jonah admitted to the crew that he was the reason for the storm because he was running from God. He told them that if they threw him overboard, the storm would stop and they would be saved. So they did. They threw him overboard!

Jonah was sunk…**BUT GOD** provided an enormous fish to swallow the prophet, and for three days and nights, Jonah was in the belly of the fish—plenty of time to think about his actions and repent. He cried out to God, who heard his prayer and caused the fish to spew him out onto the beach.

Even when we get ourselves into a mess, God will provide a way of escape. It may seem impossible and unbelievable, but the impossible and the unbelievable are God's specialty!

You may be thrown from a secure place into some deep trouble…**BUT GOD** has an answer waiting for you!

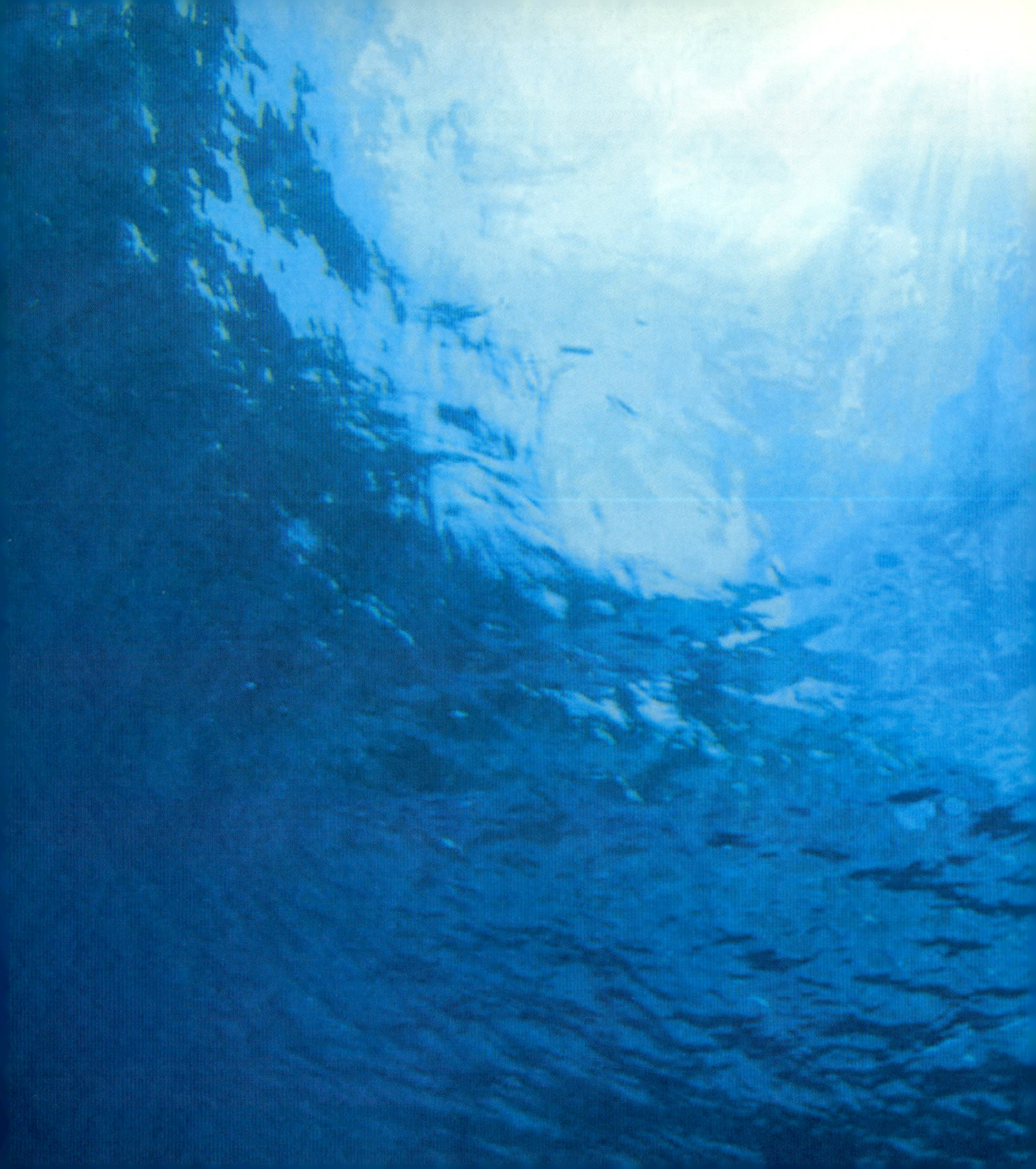

18. WHEN YOUR WORLD IS FLOODED

A flood was going to wipe out the entire world…

BUT GOD
had a lifeboat in place.

Genesis 8:1 comforts us with, "**BUT GOD** remembered Noah and all the wild animals and livestock in the boat. He sent a wind to blow across the earth, and the floodwaters began to recede" (NLT).

God was disappointed with the human race to the extent that He wished He had never even created them. He planned to wipe out the entire world…**BUT GOD** found a man named Noah, whom He could trust.

He told Noah to build something that had never been built before—an ark—for something that had never happened before—a huge flood. And Noah obeyed.

Our world is going to be wiped out...

BUT GOD has been preparing something for us so we can be saved. He asks us to do today things we don't always understand, but those very same things will be our salvation in the days that lie ahead.

Our world may be buried under a flood... BUT GOD has provided for us to be delivered!

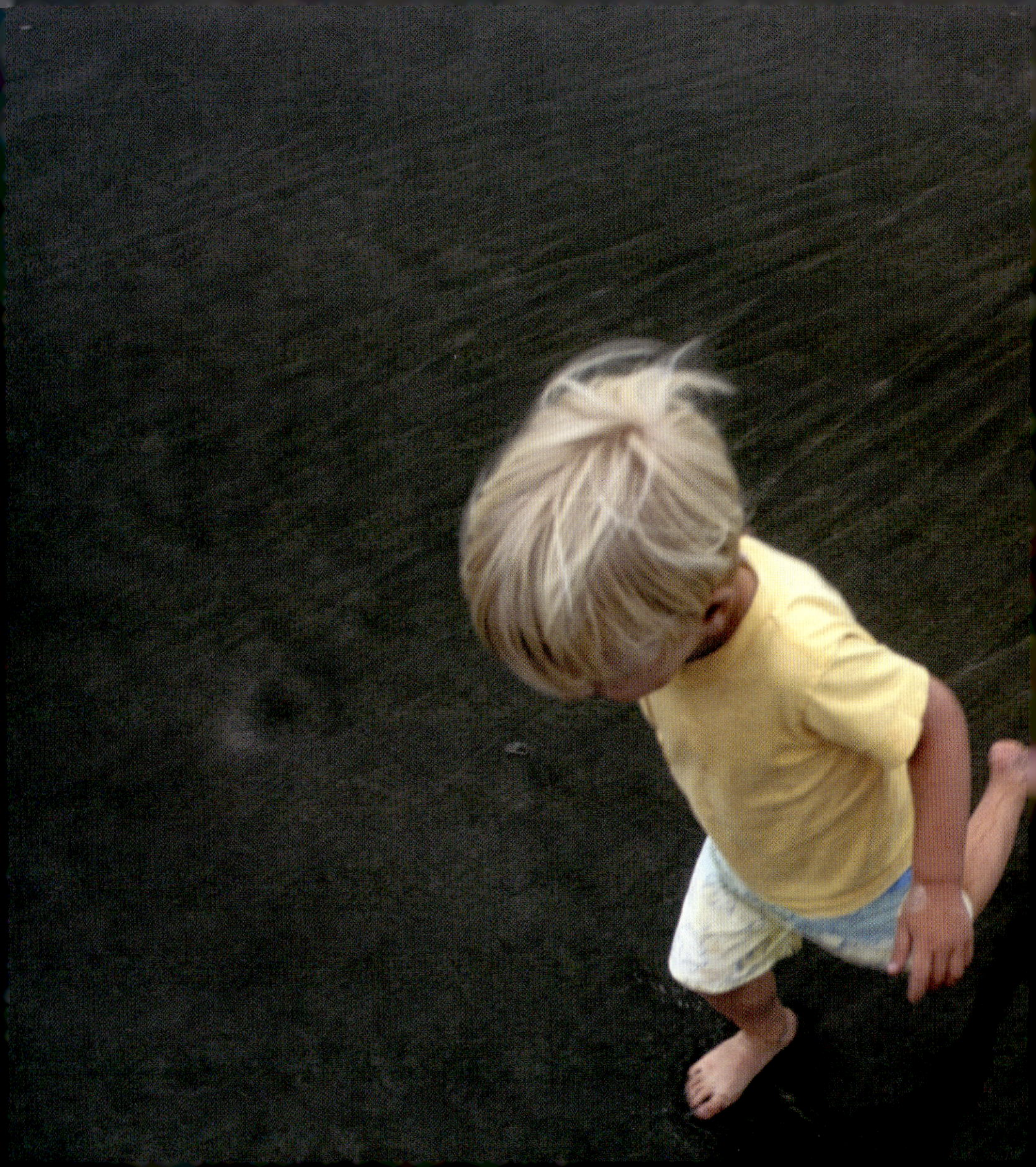

19.
WHEN YOUR CHILDREN ARE IN DANGER

You may fear for the safety, or very lives, of your children...
BUT GOD is in control of the situation.

Hebrews 11:23 reads, "By faith Moses, when he was born, was hidden three months by his parents, because they saw he was a beautiful child; and they were not afraid of the king's command."

The king of Egypt had ordered the death of every male child under two years of age so the Hebrew nation would not grow strong...**BUT GOD** interceded, preserving Moses.

When governments enforce laws that contradict God's laws, He will bring deliverance. This draconian law to kill every male child was averted by the quick births of the Israelite women and their God-fearing midwives.

Moses was conceived by faith-filled parents in a time of extreme danger. When they could no longer hide him from the soldiers who were killing Hebrew children, his mother placed him in a basket and set it afloat on the Nile river, committing her child into the hands of God.

The basket floated downstream and was found by Pharaoh's daughter. When she saw the child, she immediately fell in love with him. She rescued him from the water and asked Miriam (Moses's sister, who had been watching the basket as it floated in the river) to find a Hebrew nurse for the baby. Miriam fetched her mother. And so Moses was given to his own mother to be nursed on behalf of the princess. Moses's mother was now being paid to care for her own son, who was now being raised as the grandson of Pharaoh!

You may have a child with a life-threatening disease, or kids who are drifting into all kinds of danger…**BUT GOD** will care for them when you commit them into His hands. He will oversee the destiny of your children and provide rescue beyond your imagination.

Pharaoh may have had plans to destroy the Jewish children…

BUT GOD had other plans!

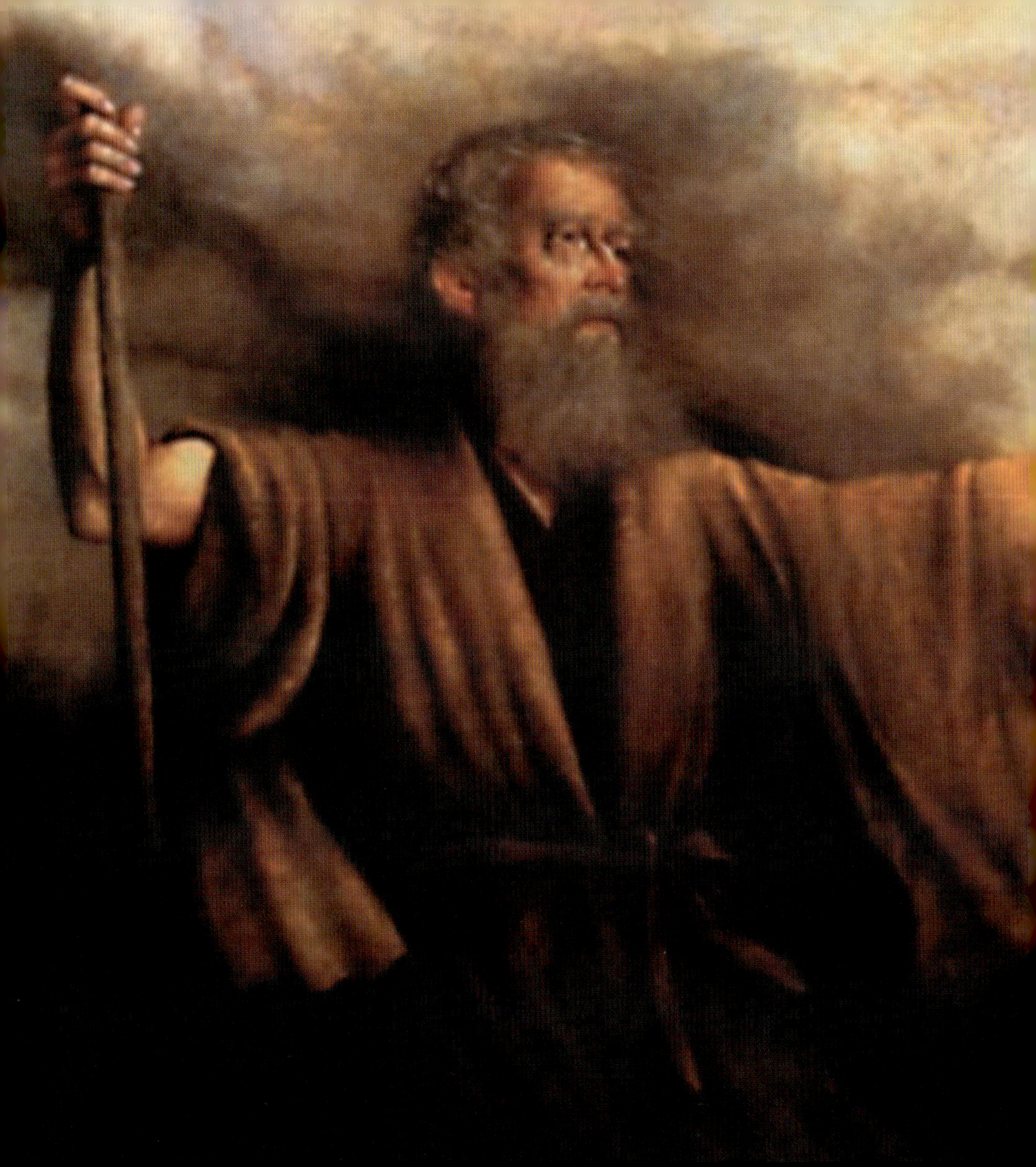

20. WHEN YOU'RE SURROUNDED BY ENEMIES

You may feel you have nowhere to turn...
BUT GOD is your Deliverer!

"Then the LORD gave these instructions to Moses: 'Order the Israelites to turn back and camp by Pi-hahiroth between Migdol and the sea. Camp there along the shore, across from Baal-zephon. Then Pharaoh will think, "The Israelites are confused. They are trapped in the wilderness!" And once again I will harden Pharaoh's heart, and he will chase after you. I have planned this in order to display my glory through Pharaoh and his whole army. After this the Egyptians will know that I am the LORD!'" (Exod. 14:1–4, NLT).

After Moses delivered the Hebrew slaves out of Egypt, they were chased down by the mighty army of Pharaoh. At the Red Sea they were stopped—not by the army, but by what seemed to be an impossible circumstance: hemmed in by a desert to the south, mountains to the north, a ferocious army behind them, and an impossible stretch of ocean in front of them.

BUT GOD...

How many times do we find ourselves with nowhere to turn except to God? He will allow us to be cornered, simply to get our attention. Even though it seems there is nowhere to turn and nowhere to go, know this: there is a way through! Somehow, some way, God will make it possible for us to get through impossible situations.

The Lord told Moses to lift his rod over the ocean in front of them. This is like holding out the name of Jesus over whatever is blocking our way. God is not intimidated by the very things He created. He who made the ocean can also part it. He did divide the sea that day for Moses and the Israelites, and three million people walked across on dry land.

And then, the very thing that was the Israelites' deliverance became the enemy's destruction. When Pharaoh's forces tried to follow on the pathway God had given His people, the walls of water collapsed and they were drowned.

NEVER FORGET THE GOD FACTOR: You may be surrounded… BUT GOD is making a way!

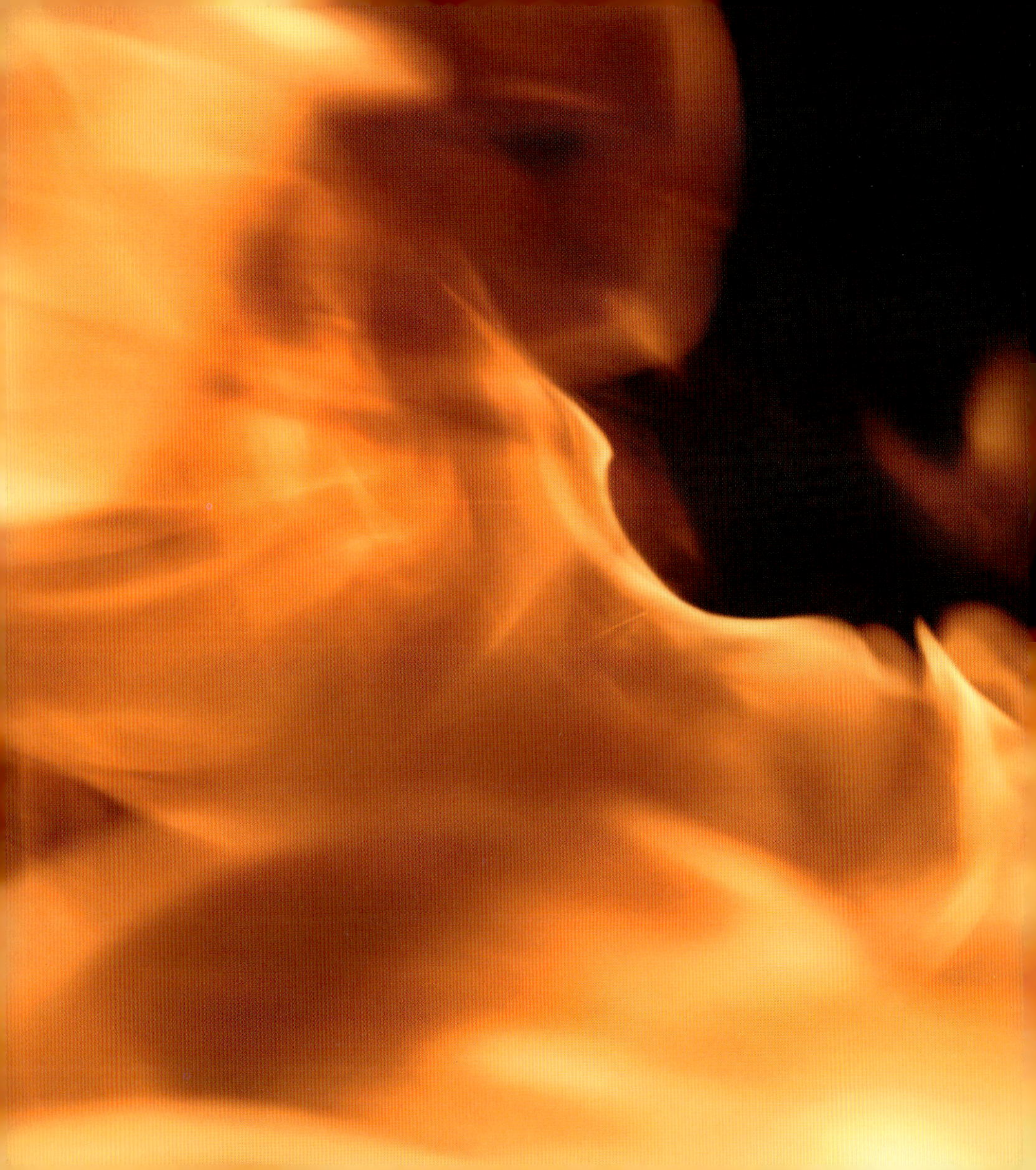

21. WHEN YOU FEEL LIKE YOU'RE GOING DOWN IN FLAMES

You may sometimes get engulfed by the flames...
BUT GOD is there to quench the fire!

Daniel 3:23 says, "So Shadrach, Meshach, and Abednego, securely tied, fell down into the roaring flames" (NLT).

Along with Daniel, the young Israelites Shadrach, Meshach, and Abednego were exiled from Israel by Nebuchadnezzar to live in Babylon. They were selected from among the best of the Hebrews, and they were to be trained in the arts, education, and Babylonian culture.

There came a time however, when the king required everyone in his kingdom to bow down to an enormous statue he had made. All of the nation would gather on the vast plain of Dura, where the statue had been erected.

The Hebrew boys were followers of almighty Jehovah, who had commanded that His people worship no other gods besides Him alone. They were faithful to God and refused to bow down, dedicated to the singular worship of the only true God, Jehovah.

The king was furious that his order was defied. He had the young offenders thrown into the furnace. He commanded the furnace to be heated seven times hotter than ever before.

BUT GOD...

Even the king's mighty men, who threw the boys into the fire themselves, were burned to death. But the young men were seen walking around in the fire, set free from their bonds. The king shouted out that there was a fourth person in the fire, who looked like "the Son of God" (Dan. 3:25).

The boys were called out of the flames, and the king declared there was no God like their God. He decreed that anyone who harmed these young men would be put to death. He then promoted them to high ranks in the kingdom. What threatened to be the worst situation they ever faced became their best, because they stood uncompromisingly for God—and so He stood for them.

"When you walk through the fire, you shall not be burned, nor shall the flame scorch you" (Isa. 43:2).

You may be in the flames… BUT GOD is there with you, protecting and sustaining you!

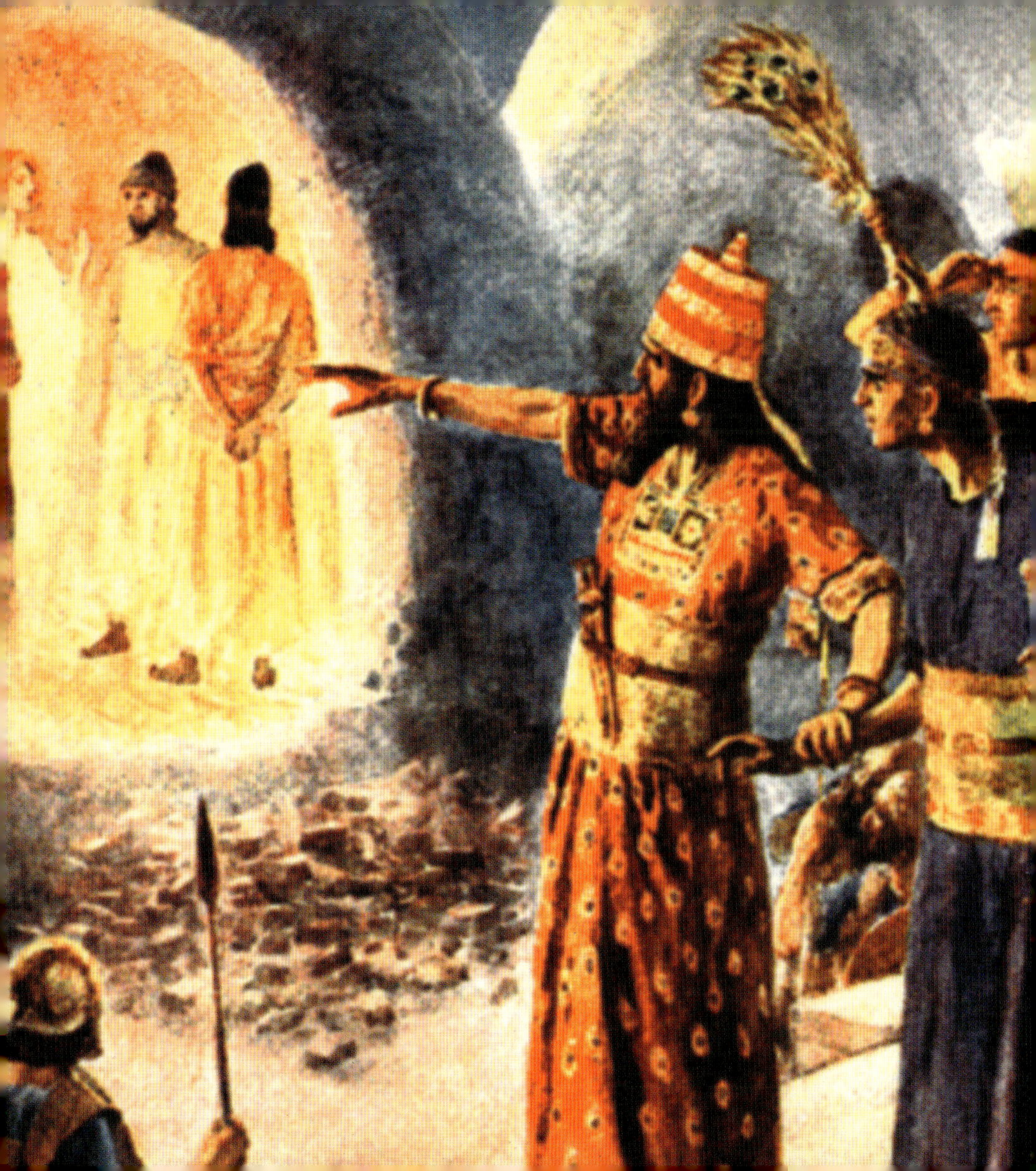

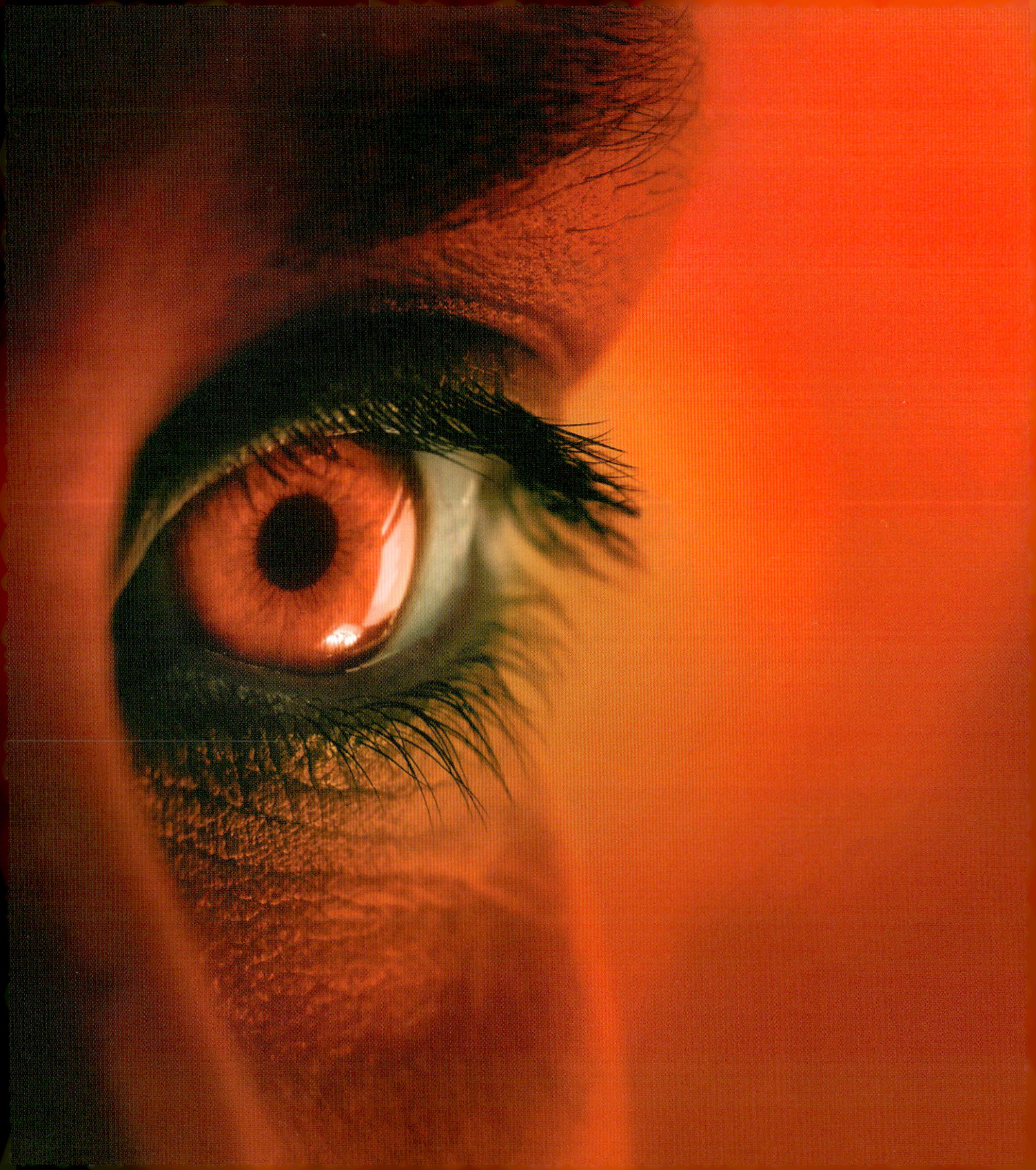

22. WHEN THE DEVIL IS ON THE PROWL

First Peter 5:8 reminds us:

"The **devil prowls around like a roaring lion** looking for someone to devour" (NIV).

The devil may be planning your demise…
BUT GOD will send His angels to protect you.

Daniel 6:22 says, "My God sent His angel and shut the lions' mouths, so that they have not hurt me."

Just like Shadrach, Meshach, and Abednego, Daniel had been exiled from Israel to Babylon as a young man. As he grew, he gained favor with the king of the land and with each successive king after him.

Israel had been conquered about seventy years earlier, and Daniel knew that God had promised to return the Israelites to their own land after seventy years had passed. So Daniel began to pray every day that God would act on His promise. Each day Daniel opened the windows of his room to pray toward Jerusalem, toward the temple, to his God—Jehovah, the only God.

Anybody as successful as Daniel will have enemies. Daniel's enemies devised a plan to destroy him. They appealed to the king's vanity and proposed a decree that no one was to pray to any other god for thirty days, or else they would be thrown into the lions' den. Daniel heard the decree, but he refused to cease praying.

When his time of prayer began, the officials entered his room, arrested him, and threw him into prison. The king loved and respected Daniel, and wished that there was some way to get around the punishment, but it was his edict, and it had to be carried out.

The king's decree stood, and Daniel was thrown to the lions…**BUT GOD** closed up the mouths of the animals, and in spite of their ravenous hunger, He stopped them from eating their prey.

"The wicked roar and growl like lions, **BUT GOD** silences them and breaks their teeth" (Job 4:10, GNT).

The devil may prowl as a lion…. **BUT GOD** will shut his mouth, break his teeth, and be your protector!

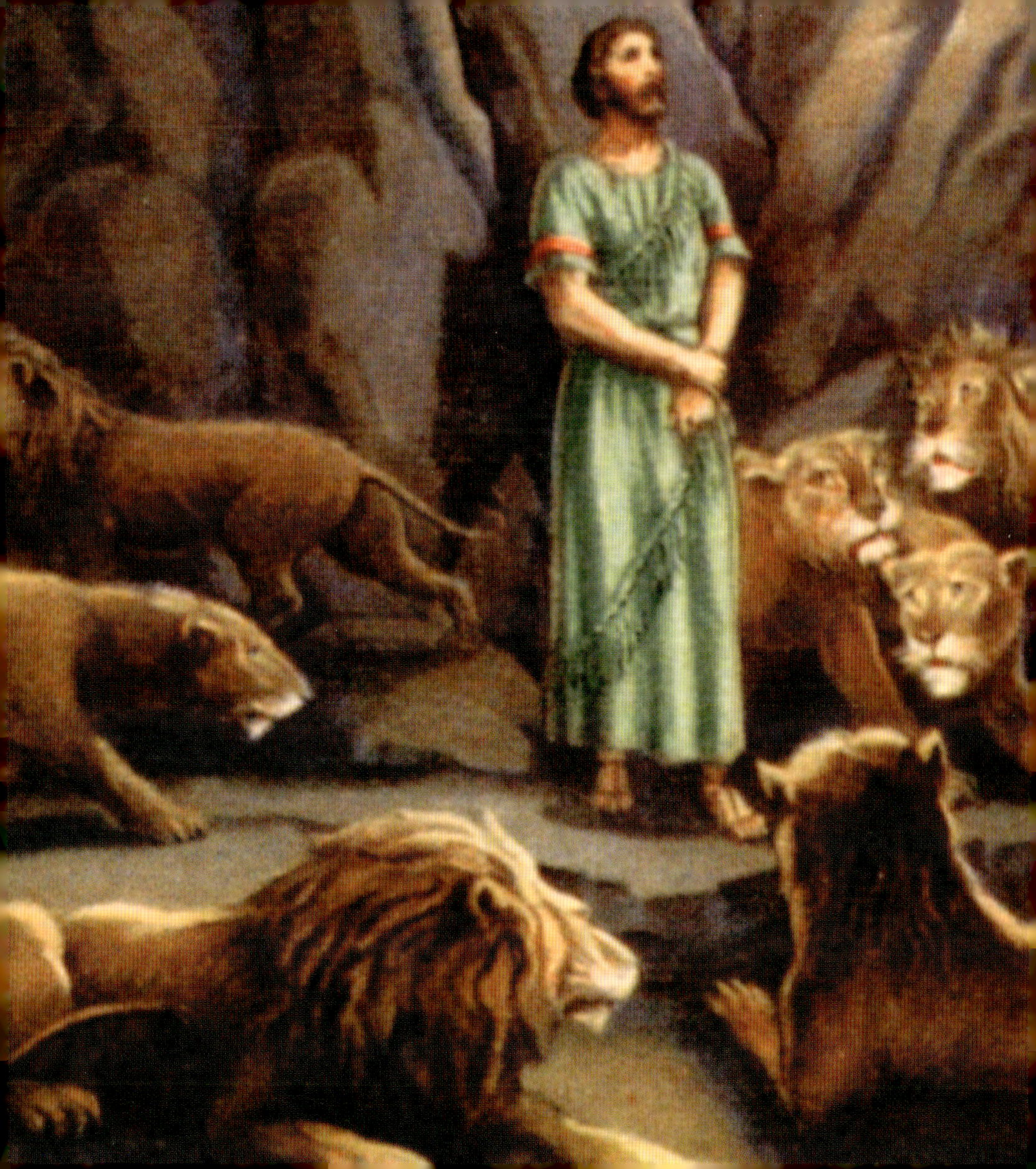

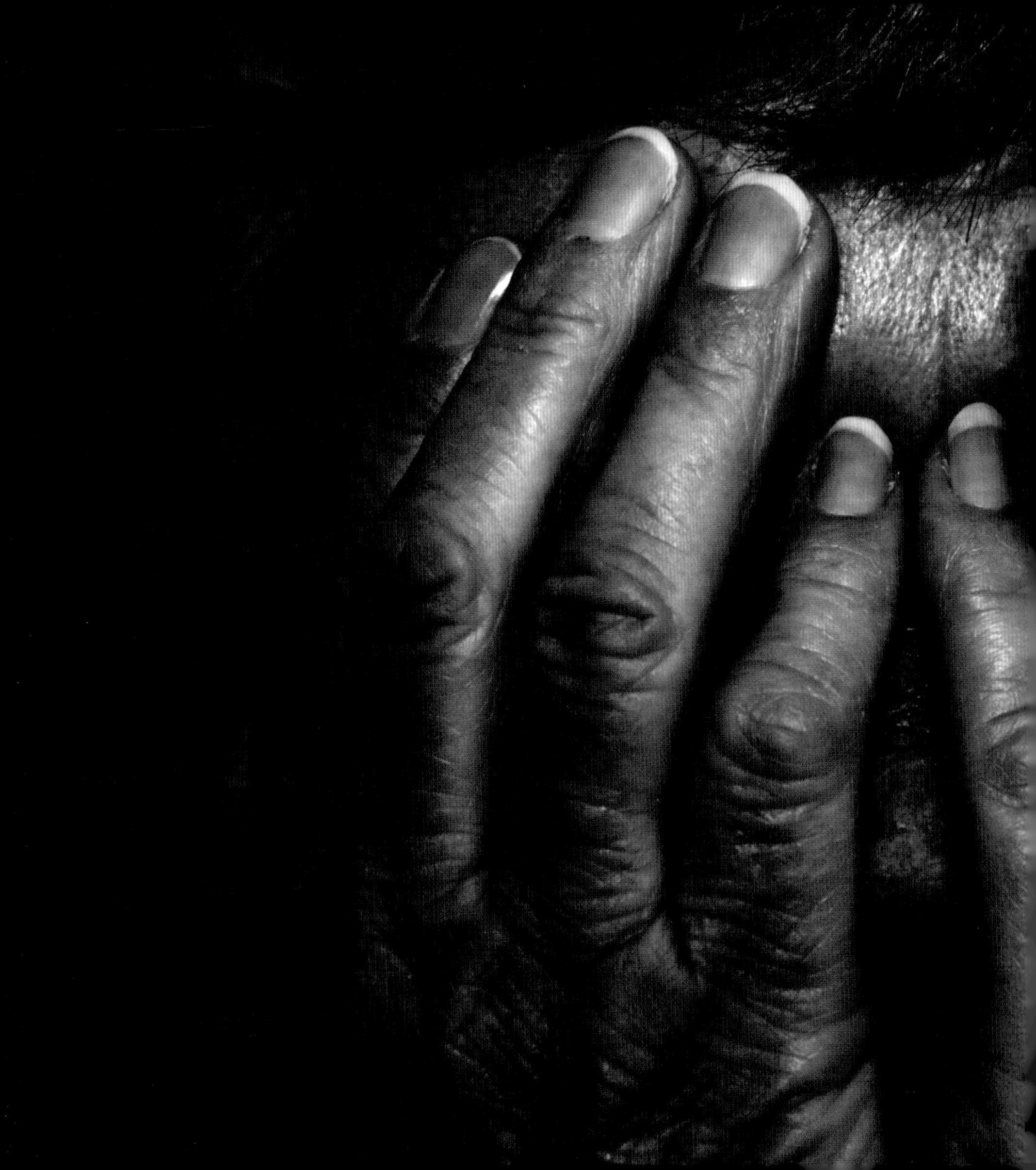

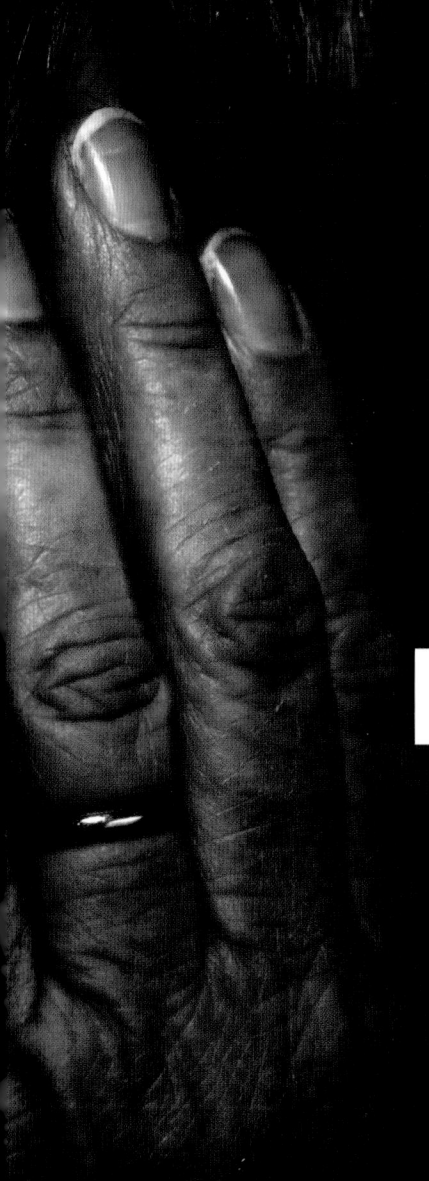

23. WHEN IT'S A MATTER OF LIFE AND DEATH

You may find yourself in life-or-death situations… BUT GOD is still the God of life!

In Genesis 50:20, Joseph told his brothers, "But as for you, you meant evil against me; **BUT GOD** meant it for good."

Joseph's brothers had tried to kill him and then sell him as a slave, but Joseph saw that it was God fulfilling a plan for his life. They had planned evil, **BUT GOD** turned it to good.

John Wesley, the man who brought enormous revival to England and whose legacy lives on throughout the world, narrowly escaped death when he was a child—one of seventeen children in his family. His father's fiery preaching had aroused the ire of the locals so much that they set his house on fire when John was only five and half years old. The house was built of dry wood and had a thatch roof. Needless to say, it burned fiercely. Everybody rushed out of the house, except young John, who was sound asleep in the attic.

When he awoke, the staircase was engulfed in flames and he could not escape. He dragged a chest up to the window and stood on it so he could be seen by the crowd below. His father thought it was all over for his son, but John managed to escape through that attic window.

His escape from death motivated John Wesley to live the rest of his life with a keen sense of purpose. He worked hard to fulfill God's call on his life, referring to himself as "a brand plucked from the fire" (Zech. 3:2).

Those who set fire to the Wesley house meant evil…**BUT GOD** used it for good.

Later, as John Wesley was preaching across England, he recorded in his journal that he was staying in a hotel, getting ready for the next day's preaching when an angry mob gathered and set fire to the hotel. He was told to leave and was forced to come out to a mob of hundreds. He walked straight to the ringleader, who stood over him with a bat in his hand ready to strike. Wesley fell to his knees and cried out to God for the soul of the man, and God answered, turning the man's heart so that he became one of John Wesley's greatest allies.

We may find ourselves in life-or-death situations...
BUT GOD will use them for good!

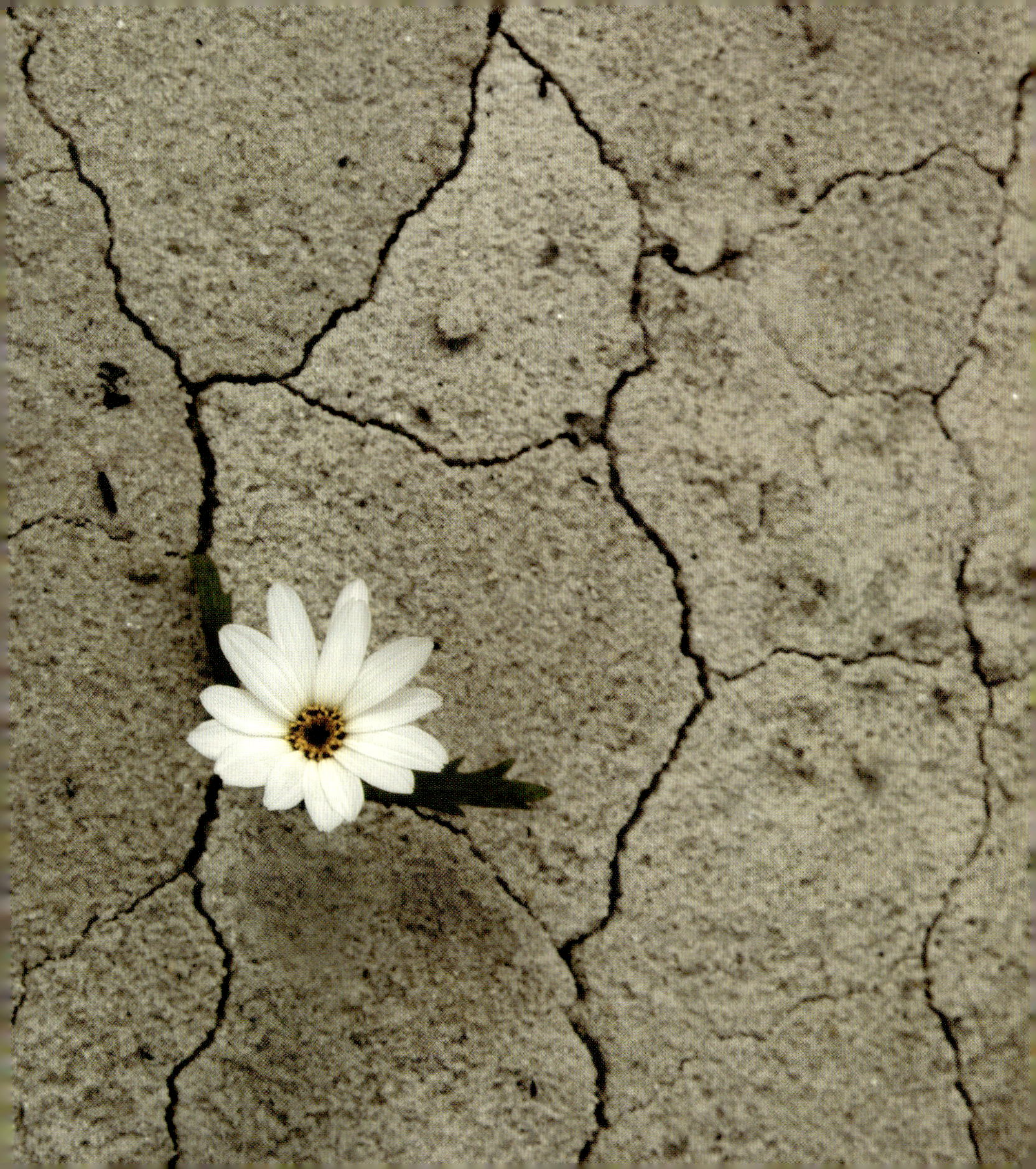

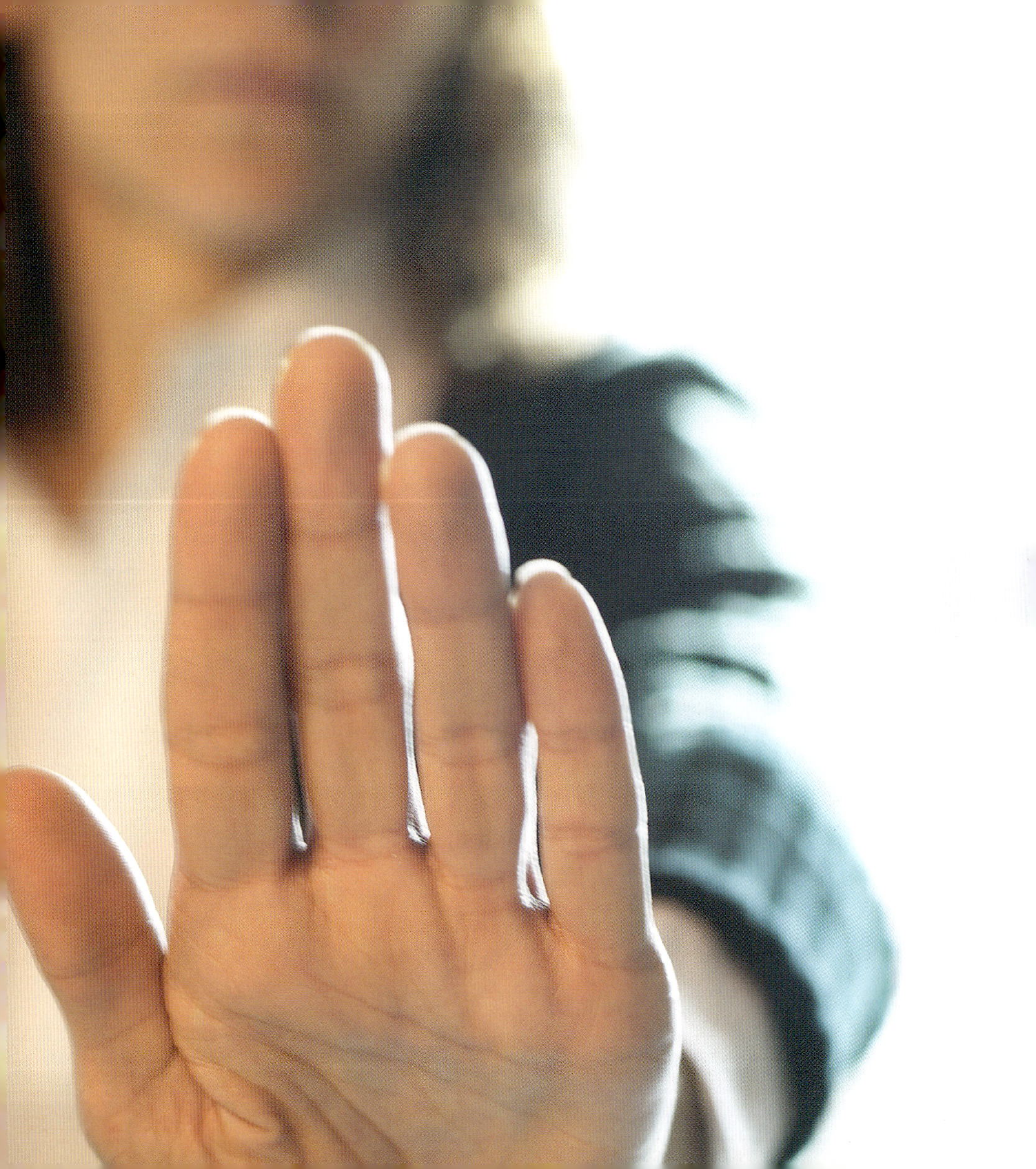

24. WHEN PEOPLE DENY GOD

People may say there is no God…
BUT GOD and His Word still remain long after those people are gone.

"The fool has said in his heart, 'There is no God'" (Ps. 14:1).

The French atheist Voltaire (1694–1778) said, "If we would destroy the Christian religion, we must first of all destroy man's belief in the Bible." He predicted that the Bible would be extinct within a century, stating that one hundred years from his death, a person would be able to find a copy of the Bible only in museums because the Bible would become a dead book!

Voltaire died in 1778. Twenty-five years after his death, the British and Foreign Bible Society was organized, and the very presses that had once been used to print Voltaire's writings were used to print copies of the Word of God.

Since Voltaire's death, millions of copies of the Bible have been printed. To this day it continues to be the number-one-selling publication in the world, selling more copies than any other book in history. The demand for Bibles increases every day. The eternal book lives on while Voltaire's works have yet to reach a complete English edition!

Just before his death, Voltaire was said to have stated, "I wish I had never been born!" The millions who have discovered life through the Scriptures celebrate the fact that they have been born again.

Voltaire is dead…
BUT GOD and His Word live on!

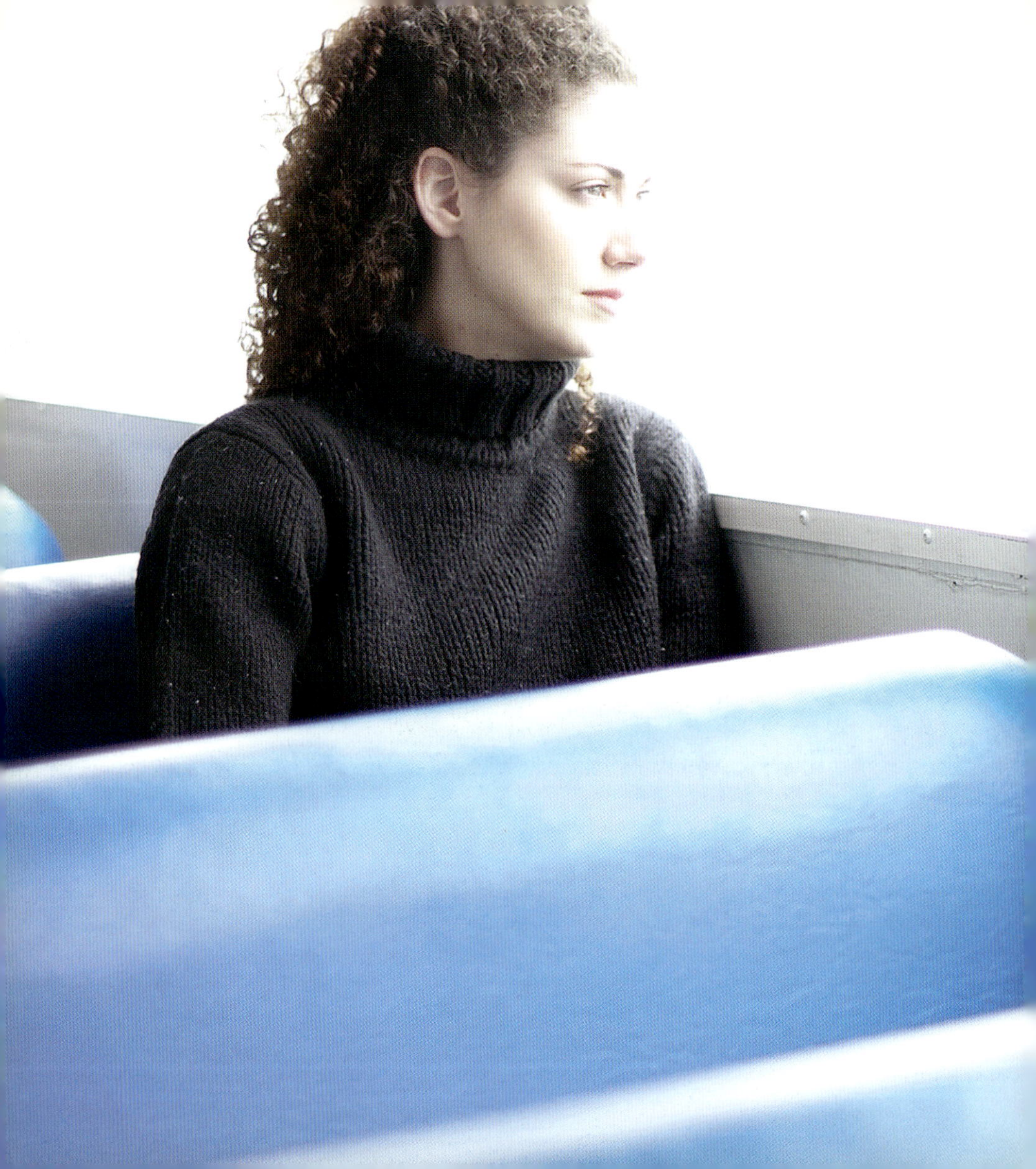

25. WHEN YOU FEEL ALONE

We may feel forsaken and alone… BUT GOD is with us!

Second Timothy 4:16–17 says, *"At my first defense no one stood with me, but all forsook me…* **BUT THE LORD** *stood with me and strengthened me."*

There are times when the people we thought would stand with us in difficult moments actually depart from us. On the worst day of Jesus's life, His closest allies and friends deserted Him.

It can be embarrassing to be associated with someone who is rejected and publicly humiliated. Paul was in prison, and many Christians of the day found it too uncomfortable to be known as an associate of his. So he was left to himself.

Most prisoners relied on the goodwill of friends to bring them food and basic necessities. There were only a few brave souls who sought out Paul in Rome and visited him. Paul was so appreciative of the Philippian church because they cared for him more than the local Roman Christians did.

Paul was so alone that, when he finally appeared before Caesar, there was no one standing with him…**BUT GOD** was with him.

When you are deserted and alone, know that God is there with you. Don't be bitter about those not standing with you; instead, be blessed by the presence of God, who is always with you.

You may feel alone and deserted…

BUT GOD will never desert you!

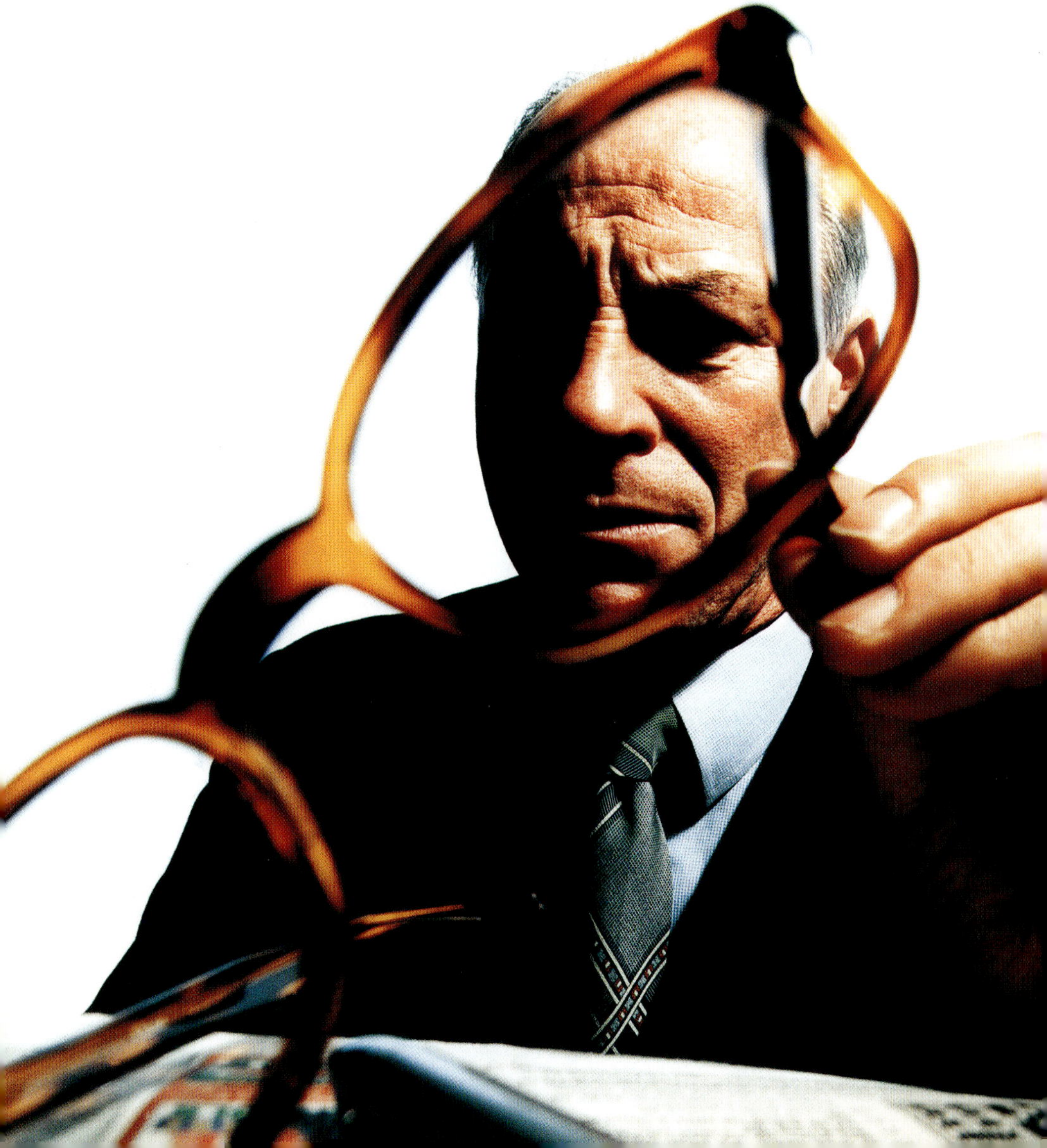

26. WHEN PEOPLE SCHEME AGAINST YOU

People may plot and scheme against us… BUT GOD will set things right.

Genesis 31:23–24 tells us, "[Laban] pursued him for seven days' journey, and he overtook him in the mountains of Gilead. **BUT GOD** had come to Laban the Syrian in a dream by night, and said to him, 'Be careful that you speak to Jacob neither good nor bad.'"

If God is for us, who can be against us?
(Rom. 8:31).

God is doing more behind your back than in front of your face. He is doing things that we are unaware of, like warning people against harming His followers.

He guides circumstances and situations so we are blessed without even lifting a finger. We are protected from an enormous amount of harm by the power of God touching other people's lives.

Right now He is working out His plan for you, making arrangements for your blessing and for your deliverance.

You may feel others plotting against you...
BUT GOD is always for us!

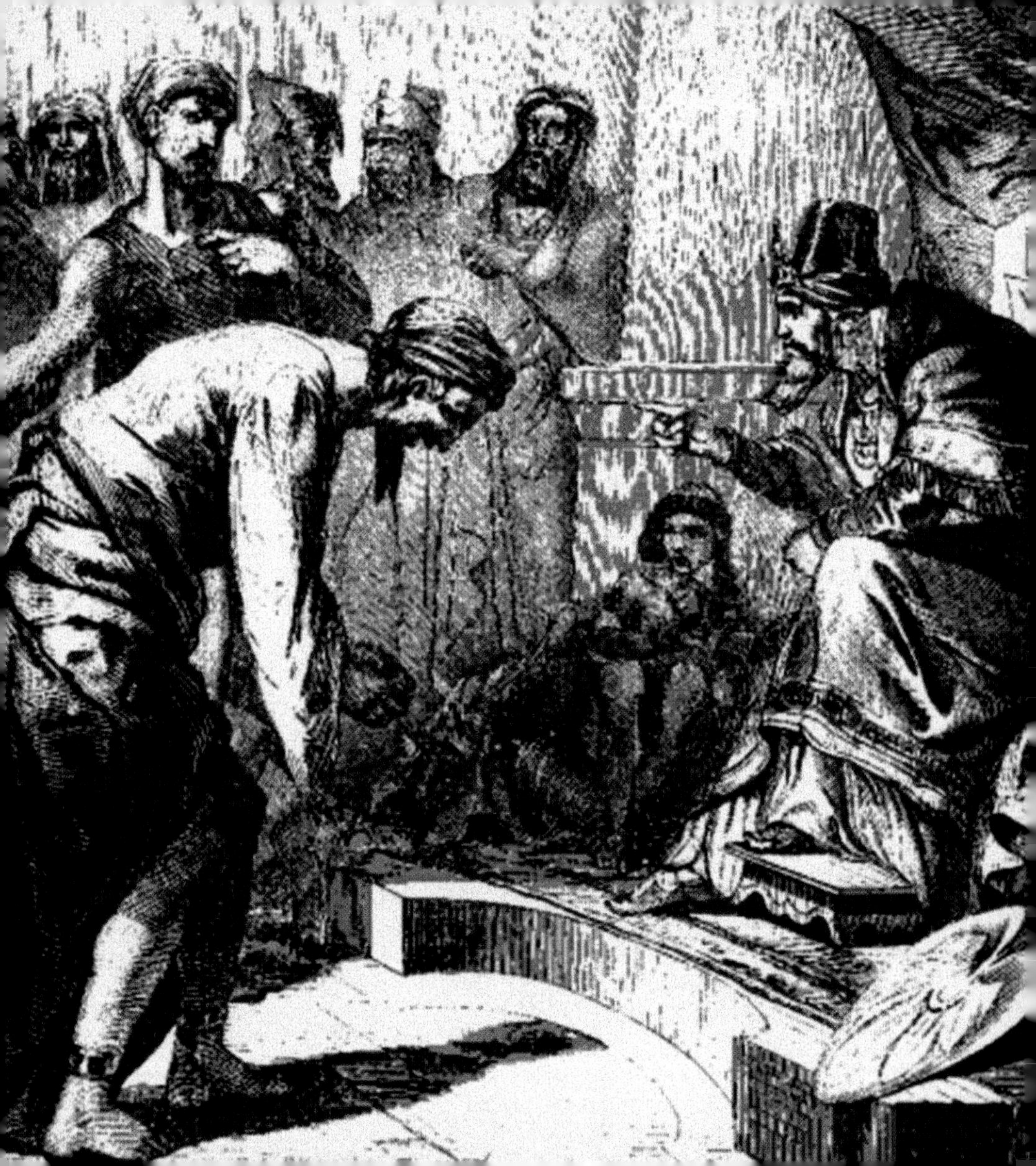

27.
WHEN A LEADER TRIES TO DESTROY YOU

Maybe a leader is trying to work against you…
BUT GOD is the ultimate leader and will work things out for good.

First Samuel 23:14 says, "And David stayed in strongholds in the wilderness, and remained in the mountains in the Wilderness of Ziph. Saul sought him every day, **BUT GOD** did not deliver him into his hand."

David had defeated the giant Goliath, and all of Israel sang David's praises more than they sang Saul's. Saul's son, Jonathan, who stood to become heir to the throne, was David's best friend, and he set out to see that David became the next king, as God had decreed through the prophet Samuel.

Saul was jealous and insecure, threatened by David's presence because the people of the kingdom loved David much more than they loved him. He knew that David was destined to become the king of Israel, but he refused to accept it. Many times he tried to kill David, hunting him across the deserts where David was in hiding.

Even though we know we have a destiny, there will always be people who will try to prevent it from coming to pass. There are those in positions who will try to stop us from succeeding. People may try to put up blockades and obstacles. The devil may try to stop you and bring you down.

BUT GOD will be there to make sure that what He has planned will come to pass!

Others may plot against you, even leaders…
BUT GOD's perfect plan will always come to pass!

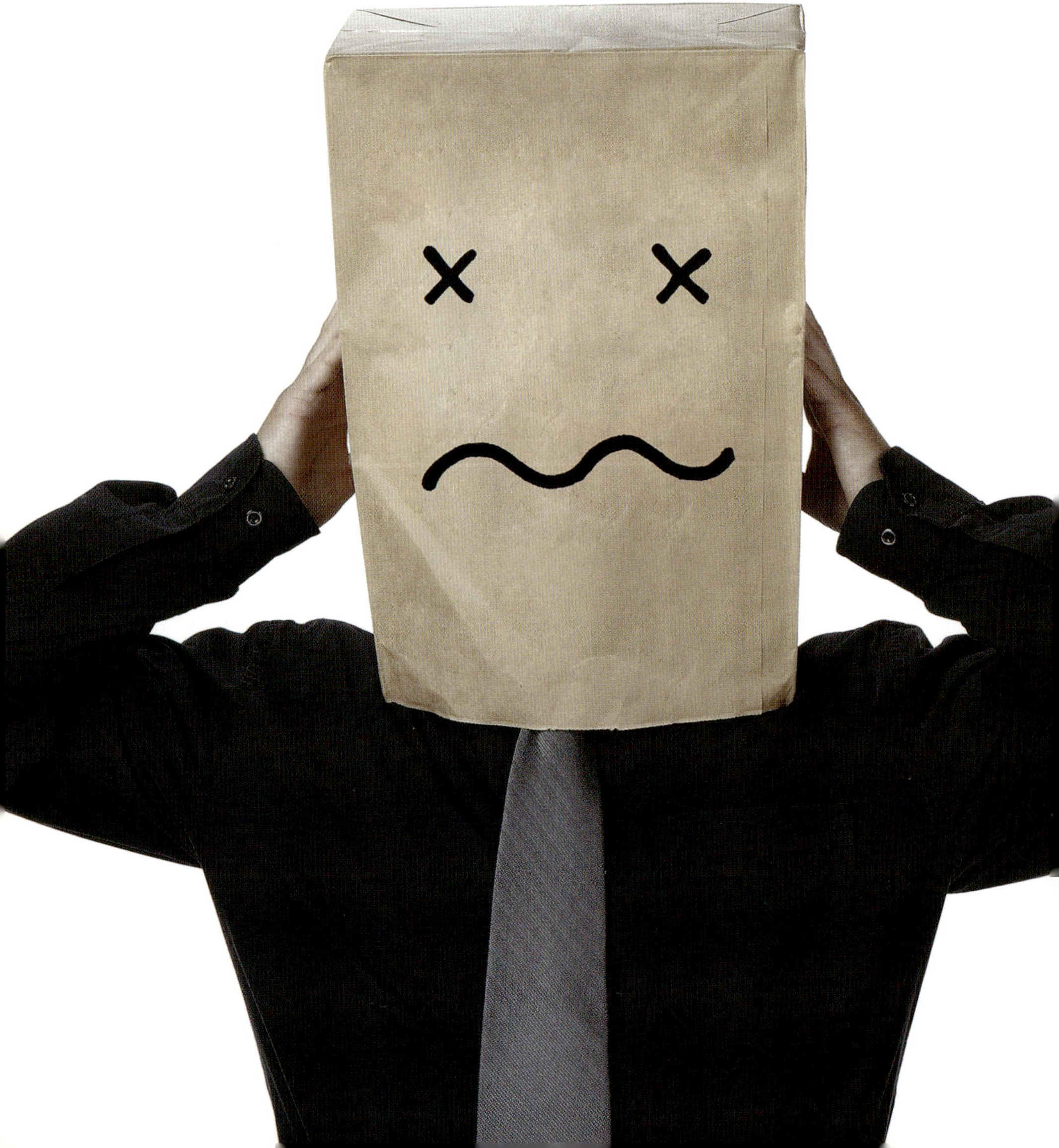

28.
WHEN YOU CAN'T INTERPRET WHAT'S GOING ON IN YOUR LIFE

We might not understand what's going on in life...
BUT GOD understands completely.

Genesis 41:16 reminds us who is the Great Interpreter: "Joseph answered, 'I cannot, Your Majesty, **BUT GOD** will give a favorable interpretation'" (GNT).

The king of Egypt had a dream he didn't understand, something he could not interpret. He knew it had great significance, but he had no idea what it meant.

All of us encounter mysteries along our journey in life. We don't know why someone died. We don't understand why we found ourselves in a predicament beyond our control. We can't explain why we made certain decisions that have disadvantaged us.

Joseph told the king that he could not interpret the dream on his own... **BUT GOD** would give a favorable interpretation. Even though he was an innocent man, mistreated by his own brothers, sold as a slave, jailed unjustly, forgotten, and deserted, Joseph maintained a great attitude.

If we lose a pure heart, we lose our ability to see. The apostle John tells us that if we hate our brother, we walk in darkness and cannot see or know where we are going (1 John 2:11). Jesus told us that the pure in heart are blessed and that they shall "see" God (Matt. 5:8).

When he heard the dream, Joseph could immediately see the translation. The dream predicted seven years of abundance, then seven years of famine. Joseph then advised the king to store up reserves in the time of abundance so he would have enough for himself and others during the famine. The king took Joseph's advice, which ultimately led to Egypt becoming the wealthiest, most powerful nation on Earth during that time.

You might have trouble reading the mysteries in your life... BUT GOD is able to interpret them, provide you with insight, and bring you to prosperity!

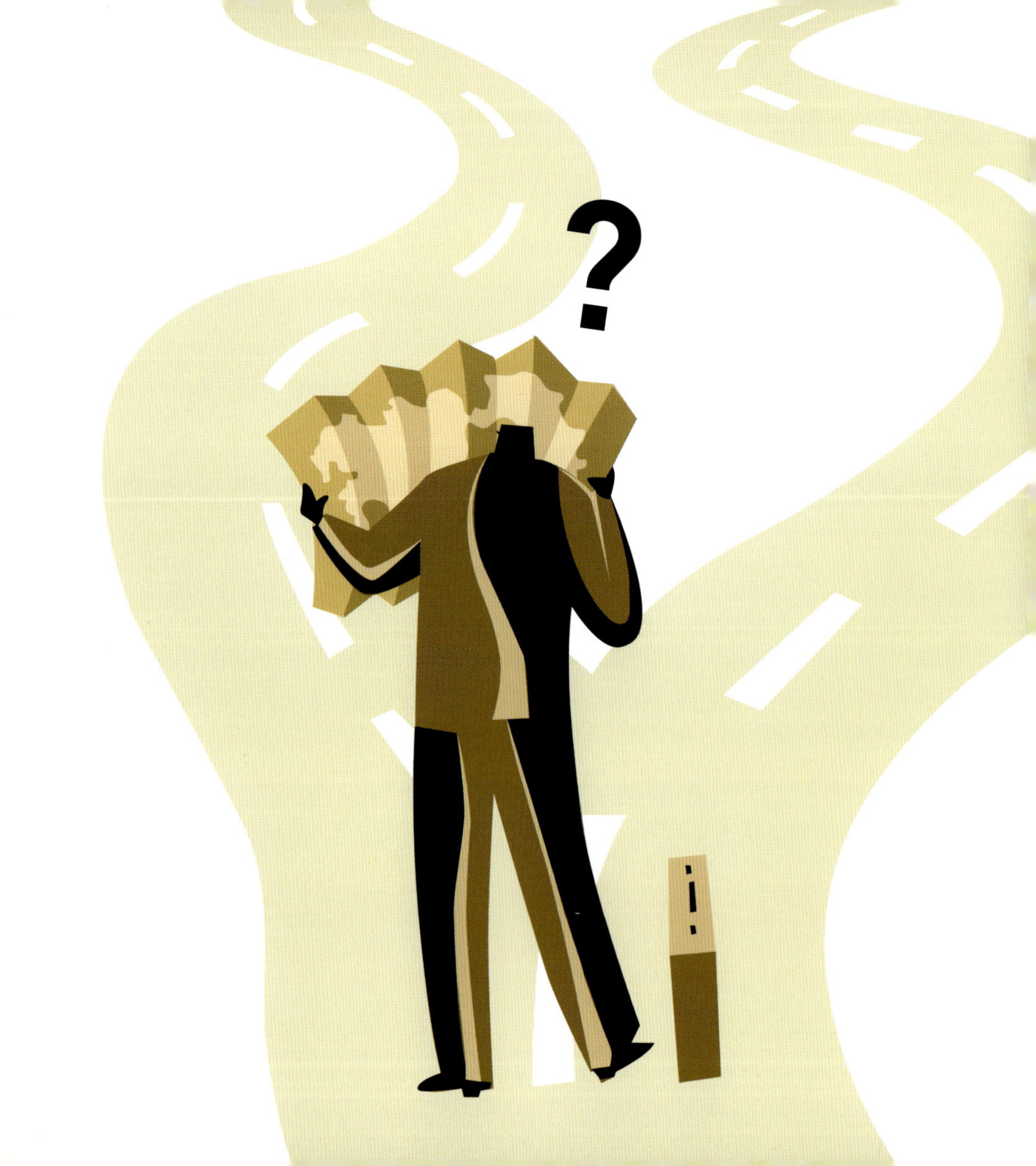

29.
WHEN YOU'RE UNSURE OF THE RIGHT DECISION TO MAKE

Sometimes you might feel confused about the proper choice to make… **BUT GOD will keep you under His wing.**

First Chronicles 16:20–21 says, "They wandered from country to country, from one kingdom to another. **BUT GOD** let no one oppress them" (GNT).

All of us feel the need for clear direction so we can make wise decisions about our future.

When we are "wandering," like the Israelites in the desert, unsure of what to do next, we are easy prey for poor decisions. We need to know that God will protect us and guide our steps.

When we are in the market for a house or a car, for example, we need to know that God will not allow people to take advantage of us. We will be guided by God as we include Him in our journey.

Walk with Him, and He will ensure that no one oppresses you.

You may feel unsure of the right path to take next…

BUT GOD will protect you each step of the way!

Application for In~~

Wherewith and heretofore of the bala~~
form~~ needed to grant~~ ~~individual or t~~
or ~~party or~~ ~~ties~~ who are not now or who ~~
be somewhat involved to a limited or exten~~
extended amount in the relief of the pain su~~
loud insistance or even not so very much stu~~
otherwise distracted most individuals or eve~~
their own admission are not now nor have ~~
under financial relief from salary or week~~
their parents nor sought likewise other ~~
~~ ~~ companies, their heirs, succe~~
~~ ~~ ~~tes,~~ buddies, husb~~

DENIED

30.
WHEN PEOPLE WITH POWER ATTACK YOU

Sometimes we are opposed by those with power greater than our own... **BUT GOD** is watching over us, as Ezra 5:5 says: "**BUT GOD** was watching over the Jewish leaders, and the Persian officials decided to take no action" (GNT).

The Jews were rebuilding the temple at Jerusalem after it had laid waste for seventy years. Nehemiah and Ezra were active in renewing both the city and the people.

Local government officials resisted these men of God all the way, planning to prevent the temple from being rebuilt... **BUT GOD** was with the Jewish leaders, and no matter what the government planned, the plans never went through.

Each of us face moments when officials with more power than character decide to oppose us, whether it's a building permit we qualify for or someone from the bank telling us we can't have the loan. There are always people who will oppose us, simply because they have the power to do so—even without good reason.

Don't lose your cool in these situations.

Remember the God factor. He is able to prevent blockages in your world. If we understand that sometimes God takes more time than we want Him to, we will experience deliverance from His hand.

People with power may try to attack us…

BUT GOD
is always stronger!

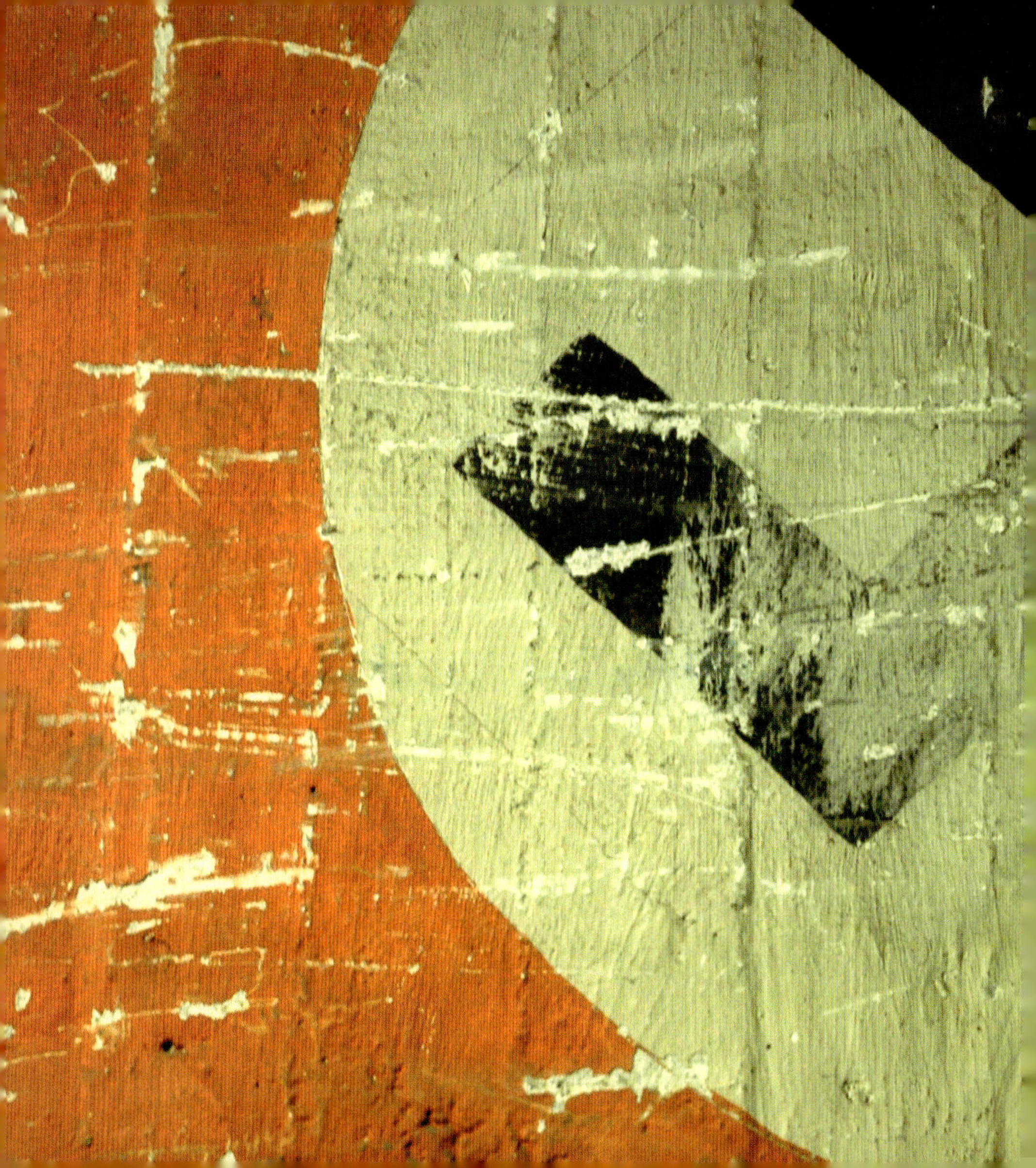

31. WHEN CRUEL PEOPLE PREY ON YOUR LIFE

When we stand for what is right, we may be attacked by people bent on doing wrong...
BUT GOD will defend us.

Proverbs 11:18 reminds us, "The wicked man does deceptive work, but he who sows righteousness will have a sure reward."

Things aren't always easy when you stand for what is right. Sometimes we may find ourselves needing to hold on to our integrity to our own disadvantage. It might cost us the deal. Or we may lose a friend. Or they may try to use legal loopholes to wipe us out.

BUT GOD will snuff out their voice and break any teeth that have been trying to snap at us.

When I was a young Christian, I was a postman. During the Christmas period, the mail increased substantially. Everyone in the office signed out at five o'clock, even when they finished much earlier.

After one o'clock we were paid triple time. Two of us were believers and felt we needed to be honest, so we signed out when we finished, rather than at five o'clock like everyone else. We took a lot of heat from fellow workers, because it made them look bad. Even the boss called us in and asked us to sign the book like everyone else. We apologized for the problem we were unintentionally causing but said we had to hold to our integrity as Christians. When the pay packets finally came out, we had exactly the same as everyone else!

I'm not sure how that happened, but I learned early that standing for Christ doesn't always disadvantage you. In fact, you will find that most people will respect your courage and will trust you before anyone else in a time of need.

Others may attack you when you stand for what is right…
BUT GOD will always honor and reward the ways of a just and honest person!

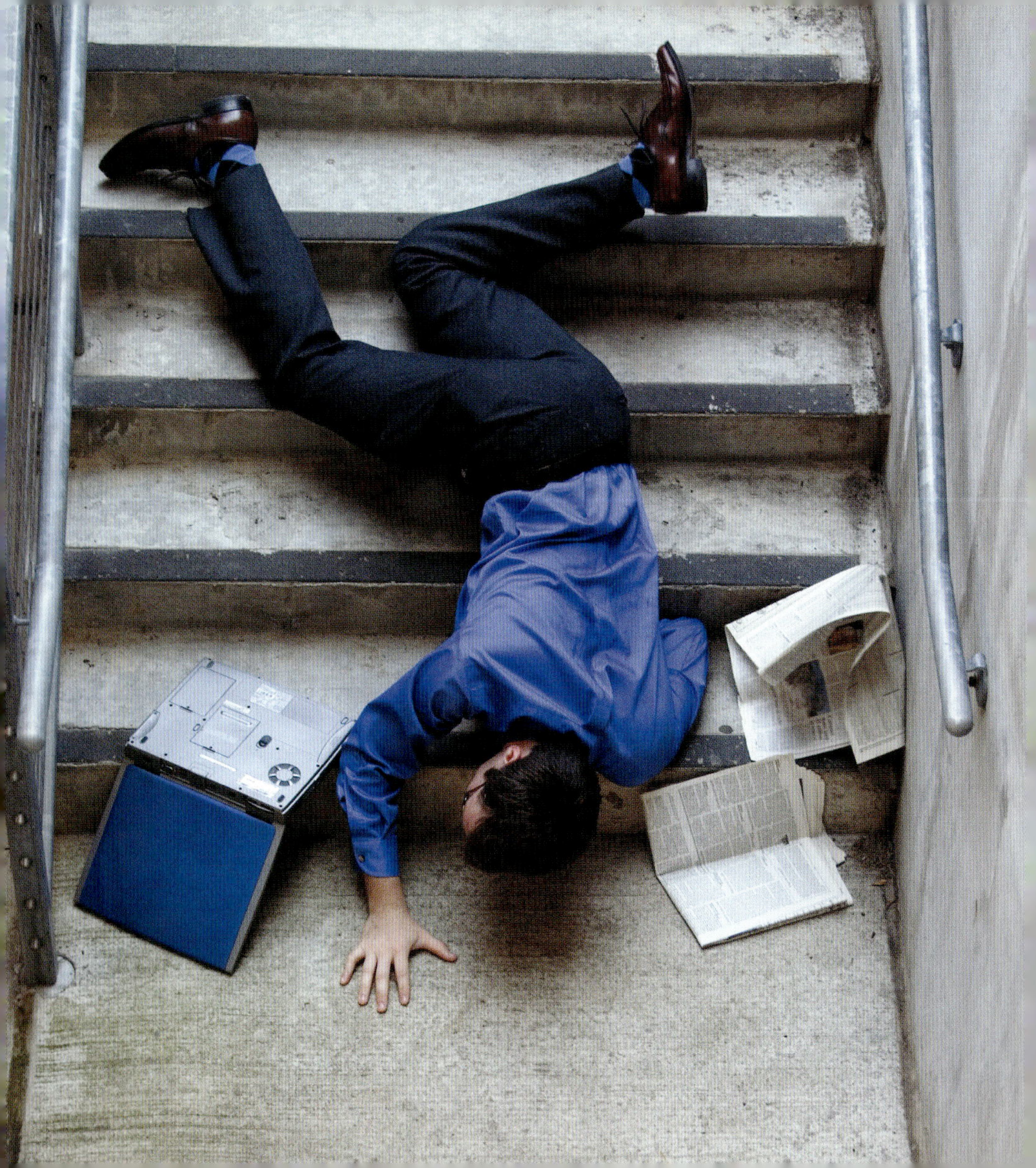

32.
WHEN EVERYONE AROUND US IS FALLING

The ungodly may fall...
BUT GOD
keeps our feet planted in His way.

"Yes, that's all the joy evil people have; others now come and take their places. **BUT GOD** will never abandon the faithful" (Job 8:19–20, GNT).

When people around us are losing their places in life, God will ensure that we are immovable. If we are faithful to Him, He will not abandon us during times of instability.

Others may be shaken out of their places in life, lose their jobs, miss out on opportunities—but the faithful will be rewarded. God will not desert us in our time of need!

When Jesus was dying on the cross, He felt like God had abandoned Him, to the point that He even cried out to God, "Why have you forsaken me?" (Matthew 27:46 NLT)… **BUT GOD** had not forsaken Him.

The emotional and spiritual pain Jesus experienced here was immense. He felt deeply disconnected from God in His soul as He bore our sin and took on Himself what we experience.

Jesus had never known separation from God. **Most people live their entire lives distant from God, but for Jesus, this was the ultimate pain.**

Yet the Scripture assures us that God will never abandon the faithful, no matter what our feelings may tell us. **His Word declares that He will not ever leave us or abandon us.** And we can see this by the fact that while others may be losing their places in life, we are not.

Those around us may fail and fall...

BUT GOD

upholds the way of the righteous!

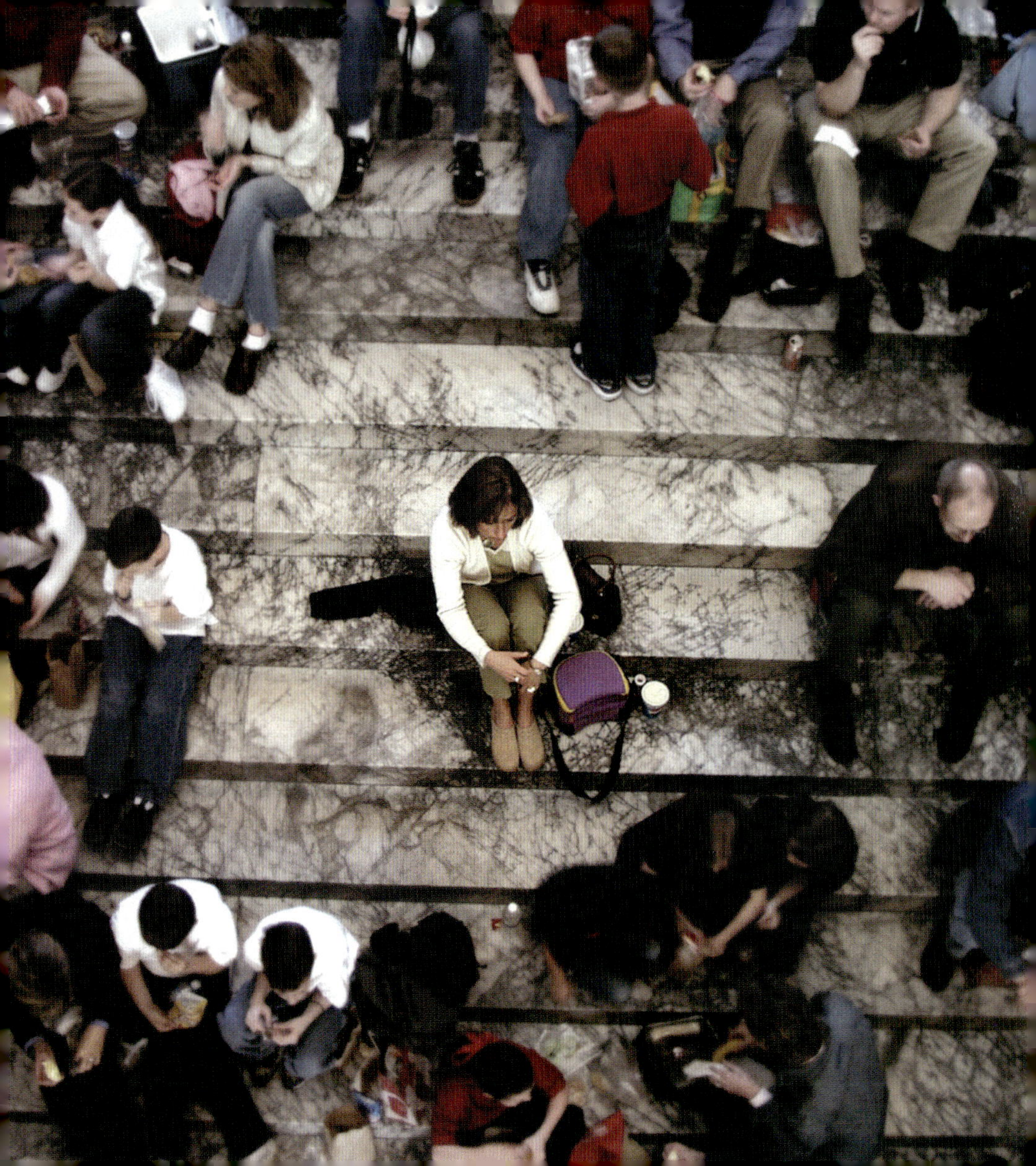

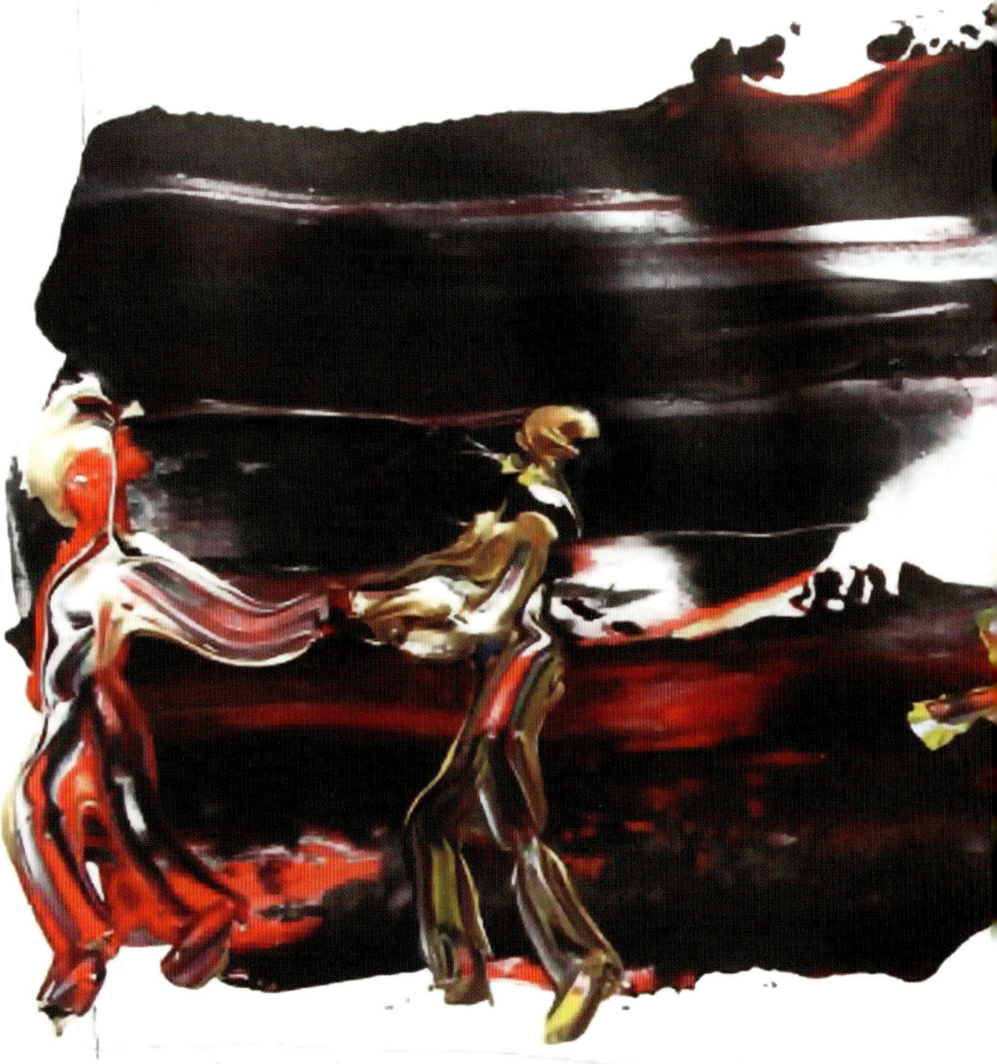

33. WHEN YOU'VE DONE WRONG

We all do wrong…
BUT GOD extends unending and immeasurable mercy when we repent.

Job 33:27 encourages us: "I have not done right, **BUT GOD** spared me" (GNT).

All of us have done wrong at some time. Some of us have done more wrong than others, but no matter what amount of wrong we have committed, we are all sinners before God.

A little sin and a lot of sin are still sin, and we all need His mercy and forgiveness as much as the next person

The key to receiving God's mercy is found in what Job said: "I have not done right." This is what repentance looks like, and repentance is the foundation to a relationship with God.

When we are prepared to confess our wrongs to God, we will find forgiveness. But until we confess, forgiveness cannot be ours.

Without repentance, neither His forgiveness nor the blood of Jesus are effective in cleansing us and restoring us to a relationship with Him. Why? Because without repentance, we are, in effect, refusing His grace. Our pride and fear can stop us from repenting, but once we do repent, we will find ourselves set free from the power of darkness and from the urge to sin.

Repentance needs to be regular in our lives, a habit like bathing or brushing our teeth. As we maintain a soft heart and a clean life, we walk with God and find ourselves spared from all kinds of disasters because of the mercy of God in our personal world.

Every single one of us does wrong…

BUT GOD does wonders in the life of a repentant soul!

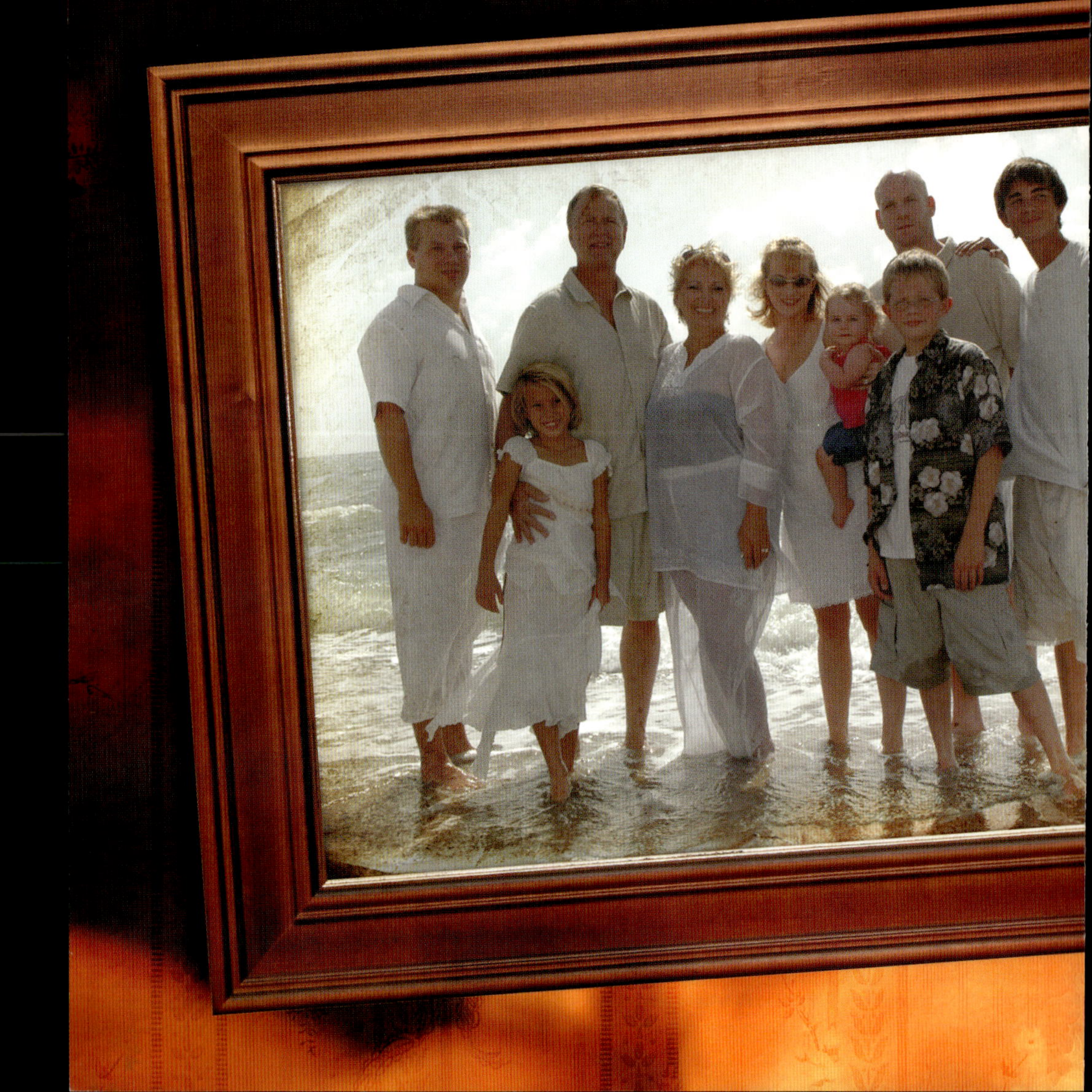

34. WHEN YOUR FAMILY FEELS THE HEAT

Your family might be in trouble…
BUT GOD has answers.

Genesis 19:27–29 says, "The next morning Abraham was up early and hurried out to the place where he had stood in the Lord's presence. He looked out across the plain to Sodom and Gomorrah and saw columns of smoke and fumes, as from a furnace, rising from the cities there. **BUT GOD** had listened to Abraham's request and kept Lot safe, removing him from the disaster that engulfed the cities on the plain" (NLT).

Abraham's nephew, Lot, was under threat. The angel of death was ready to wipe out Sodom and Gomorrah, where Lot lived. Even though Lot's family was not living right, Abraham prayed, asking God to spare his nephew.

When the smoke came, it looked hopeless.
BUT GOD spared Lot.

You need to know that when your family is being destroyed by strife, God has the answer.

Your children may be running with the wrong crowd,
BUT GOD can put them where they need to be.

Your father or mother may be sick,
BUT GOD can bring them health.

Your marriage may be breaking down,
BUT GOD can mend what is broken.

It doesn't matter what your family situation is.
God is God over it all.

The ones you love may be in difficult situations, and your life may seem to be going down in flames…BUT GOD will work it out better than you can ever imagine!

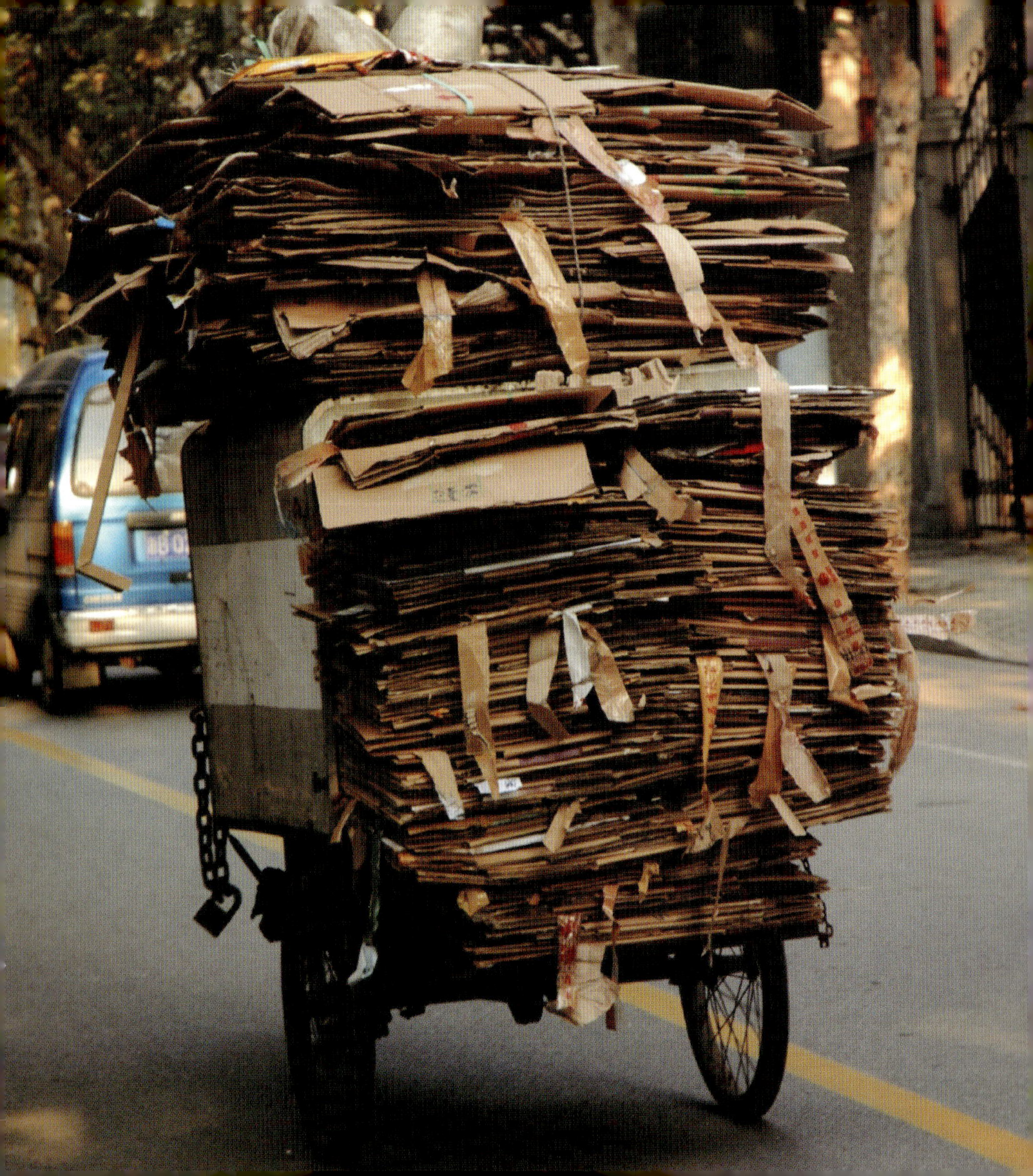

35.
WHEN YOU'RE FACING ENORMOUS PROBLEMS

We might face giants in life…

BUT GOD is
larger
than them all.

"That was also regarded as a land of giants; giants formerly dwelt there. But the Ammonites call them Zamzummim, a people as great and numerous and tall as the Anakim. **But the LORD** destroyed them before them, and they dispossessed them and dwelt in their place" (Deut. 2:20–21).

When the Israelites arrived at the borders of Canaan, their Promised Land, they found it infested with giants, and despite all God had already brought them through, they became fearful and demoralized. They refused to enter the land as God had told them. They turned back in fear, disobedience, and unbelief. They looked at the giants and simply could not believe they were equal to the task of defeating them.

All of us will face gigantic circumstances, where we feel we have no hope of winning. **But even when we find ourselves full of unbelief, we need to refuse to go into reverse gear and become negative and unbelieving about what God can do through us.**

Statement of Charges

PAST DUE
PLEASE REMIT

FIRST CLASS MAIL
Statement

If God hates anything, it's unbelief. If He loves anything, it's faith. As soon as Joshua, the faith-filled successor to Moses, took leadership of the nation, he moved them right into their Promised Land, defeating all the giants in their path. That's the kind of faith-filled action God wants.

When we step out in faith, God will be with us and defeat the giants we are facing.

Life's giant worries may try to discourage us or send us away in fear…

BUT GOD will empower us to drive them away for good.

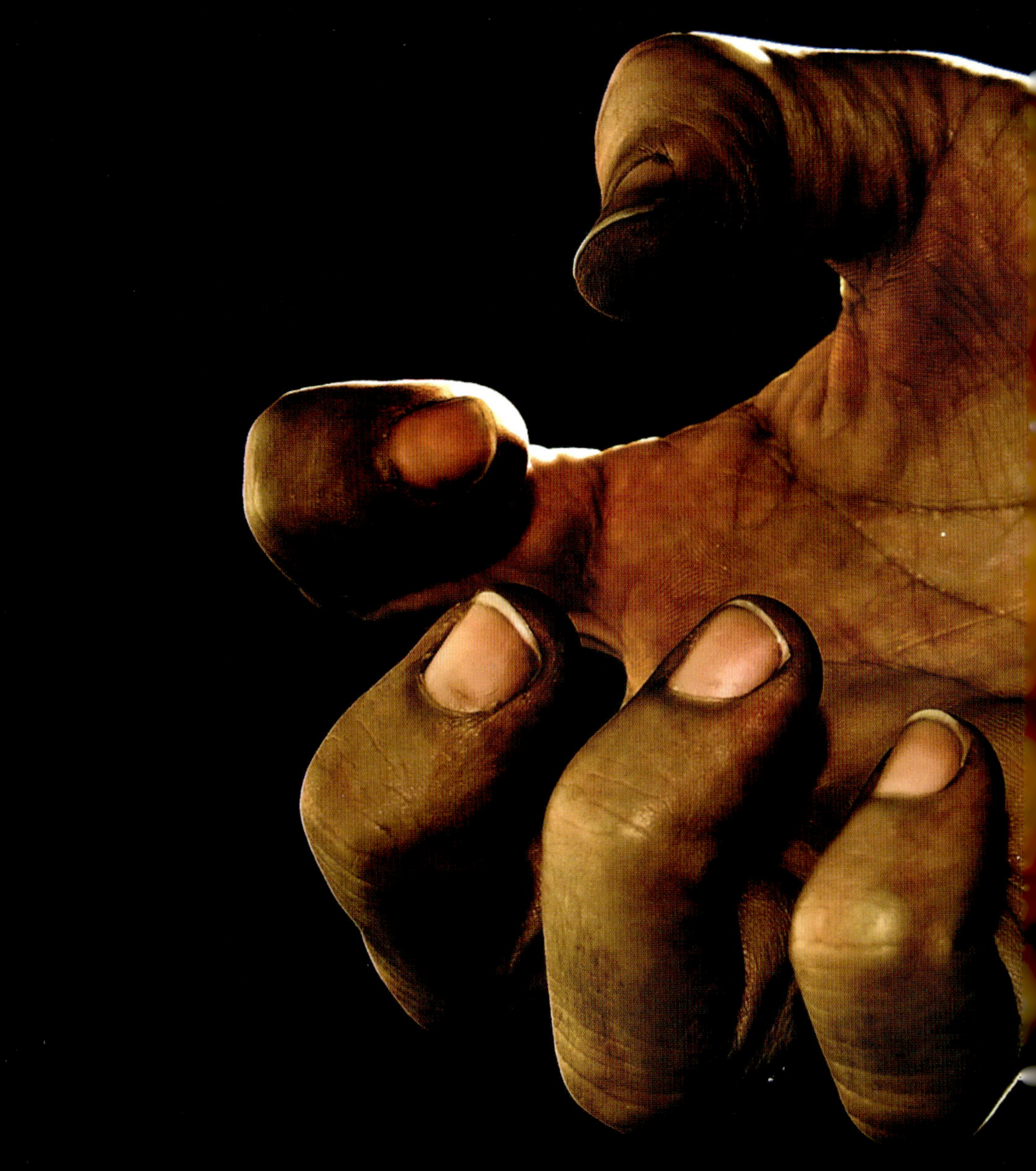

36. WHEN PEOPLE CURSE YOU

**People may curse us…
BUT GOD can turn
it into a blessing.**

> Deuteronomy 23:5 says,
> "Nevertheless the Lord your God
> would not listen to Balaam, **BUT
> THE Lord** your God turned the
> curse into a blessing for you, because
> the Lord your God loves you."

When we bring God into our problem, curses become blessings. The worst things that have happened in our lives can become the best things if we let God get a hold of them.

When you start to believe that those worst moments can be transformed into the best as you give them over to the Lord, He will do so!

When Jesus told the fig tree it would never again bear fruit (Matt. 21:18–19), the disciples called that a curse. They referred to it as the tree Jesus had cursed. He had not literally said, "I curse you," but just saying what He did brought a curse on the tree.

Many of the things people have said to us are like a curse. Parents have said their children will never make it in life. Schoolteachers have told students they are hopeless and doomed to failure. Employers have declared their workers are idiots and will always be poor. Even religious leaders have told their people they are useless.

These things are as good as a curse over people's lives—but we don't have to accept them! God can turn curses into blessings. No matter how hard people try to bring misfortune to us, God will turn it around to become a blessing.

Instead of being a victim and feeling that your past rules your life with negativity, start believing that God the Redeemer has transformed every bad thing in your life into a blessing. Believe this today!

Others may curse you…BUT GOD transforms it into a blessing!

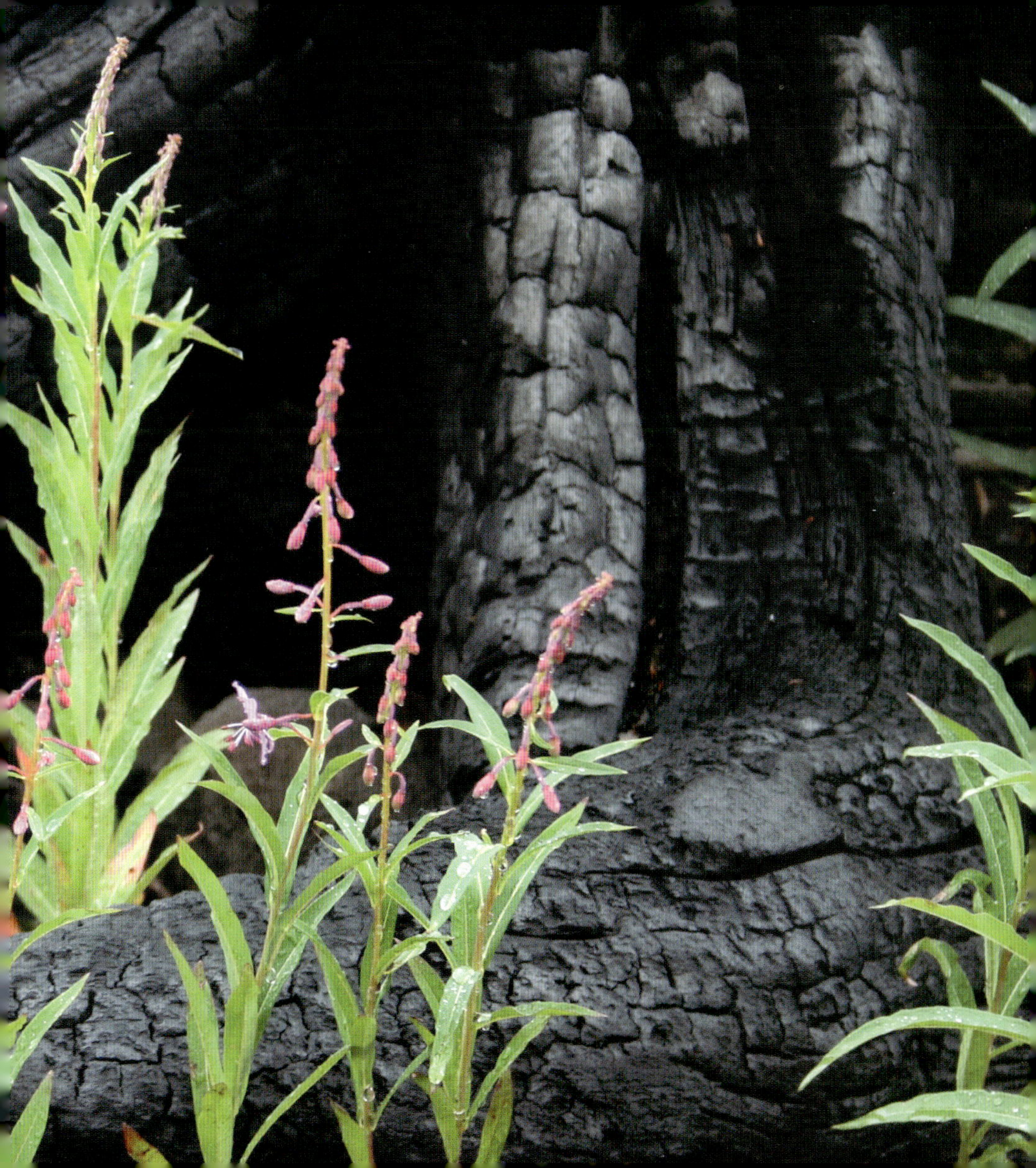

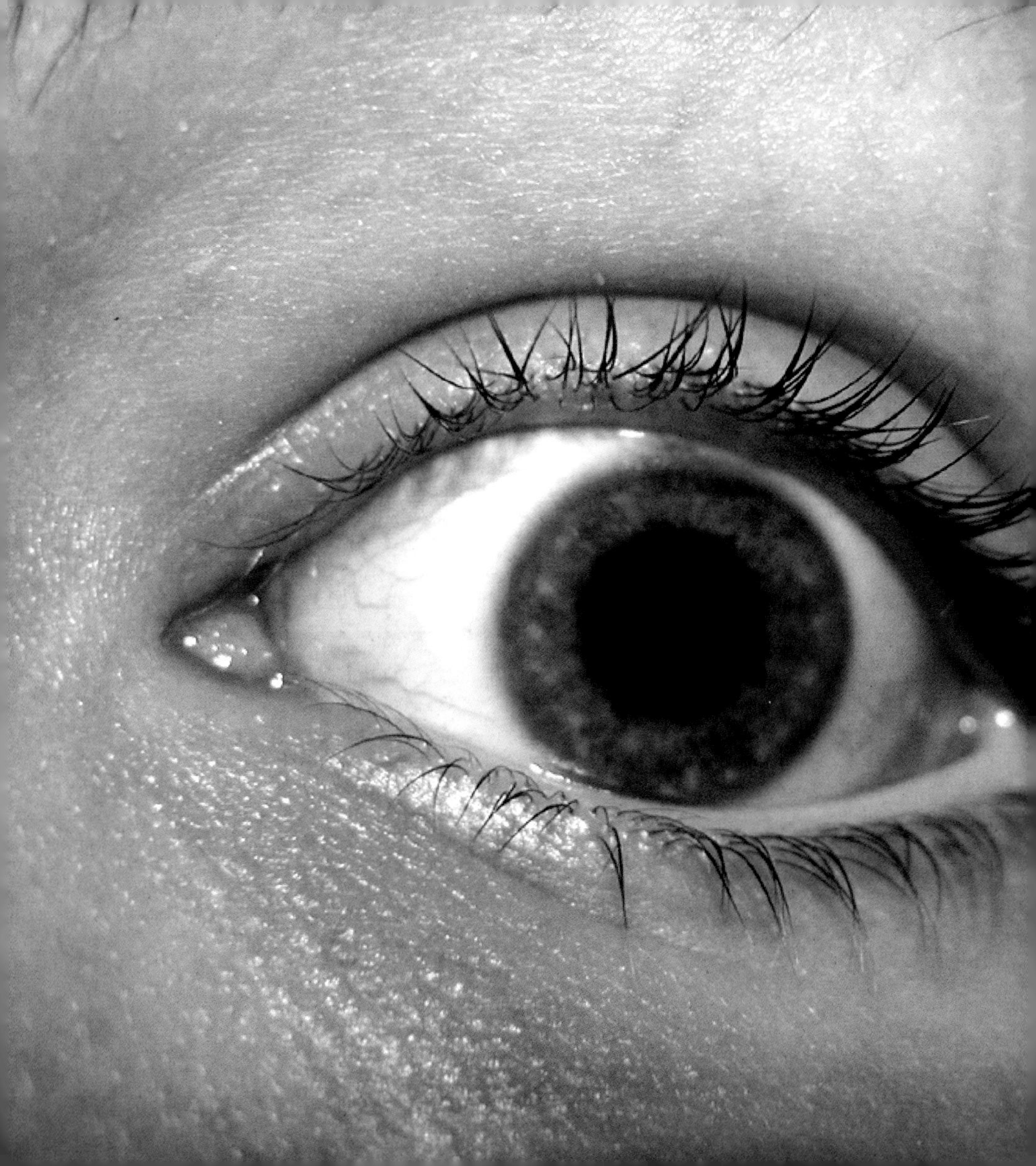

37. WHEN YOU'RE FEARFUL

We may be afraid sometimes…
BUT GOD says,
"Do not fear."

"**But the Lord** said to Joshua, 'Do not be afraid because of them, for tomorrow about this time I will deliver all of them slain before Israel'" (Josh. 11:6).

One of the greatest phrases in the world is "fear not." Say it to yourself right now: **FEAR NOT!**

Every time you are afraid, say to yourself, "'Fear not,' says the Lord!" This is one of the most faith-imparting statements you can make to yourself.

Joshua is one of the greatest men of faith, yet even he found himself fearful. All of us do. This is not a sin, but it's an opportunity to build our faith and to see God do something amazing.

Whenever your faith is stretched, you will encounter the borders of your doubt. Doubt is part of the process of faith. We know we've reached the end of our faith when we begin to doubt. It's at that point that we need to speak the Word of God. Why? Because faith comes from hearing the Word of God (Rom. 10:17).

God is the only answer to our fears, the only One who can calm them, giving us peace. Looking to Him evaporates fear.

People may be speaking fear and unbelief into your heart, **BUT GOD** speaks faith to you! Hear His Word louder than any other words. His power transmits in the atmosphere of faith.

We may be fearful…
BUT GOD
calls us to "fear not."

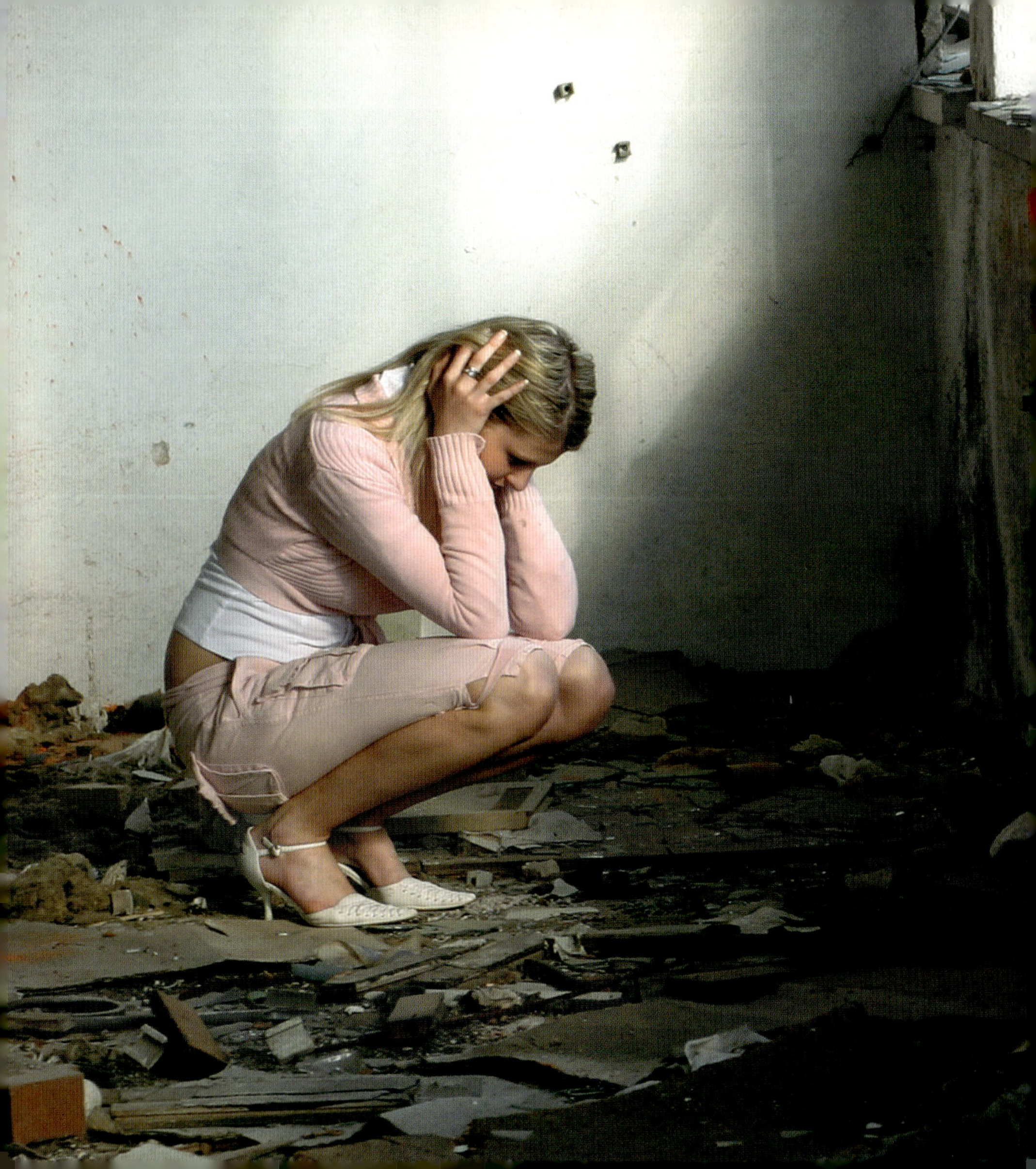

38. WHEN YOU'RE VULNERABLE

You may feel weak and vulnerable…
BUT GOD will protect and defend you.

"He delivered me from my strong enemy, from those who hated me; for they were too strong for me. They confronted me in the day of my calamity, **but the Lord** was my support" (2 Sam. 22:18–19).

There are days when we are unequal to the problems we face. Our enemies are just too strong, and we seem unable to do anything about the difficulties surrounding us.

Sometimes people and life play unfairly. On the day of David's vulnerability, his enemies took advantage of his weakness and attacked him when he was down. It's a terrible time when you're weak and more problems come. **It's a bad day when you're already down and people take advantage and attack you. That is the time when God will be your support. He will deliver you. Look to Him.**

In the day of Job's calamities, his friends began accusing him of hidden sins. They showed no mercy, even though he had shown great mercy throughout his life. He eventually came through his calamity, and God rebuked his friends. As Job emerged from his disasters, he prospered twice as much as he had before. When he prayed for his friends who had attacked him when he was down, he revealed the gracious character of his soul.

You may feel vulnerable to the problems confronting you…

BUT GOD will be your strength!

FREE NEWSLETTERS
TO HELP EMPOWER YOUR LIFE

Why subscribe today?

- **DELIVERED DIRECTLY TO YOU.** All you have to do is open your inbox and read.

- **EXCLUSIVE CONTENT.** We cover the news overlooked by the mainstream press.

- **STAY CURRENT.** Find the latest court rulings, revivals, and cultural trends.

- **UPDATE OTHERS.** Easy to forward to friends and family with the click of your mouse.

CHOOSE THE E-NEWSLETTER THAT INTERESTS YOU MOST:

- Christian news
- Daily devotionals
- Spiritual empowerment
- And much, much more

SIGN UP AT: **http://freenewsletters.charismamag.com**

Phil Pringle ARTWORK

Dr. Phil Pringle is the senior minister of Christian City Church Oxford Falls in Sydney. Started by Phil and his wife, Chris, Christian City Church has become a significant Australian church. An entire movement of vibrant churches has been birthed as a result of Phil's leadership and vision.

Phil has painted for over thirty years and actively exhibited in the past eight years. He studied at the Ilam School of Fine Art in Christchurch, New Zealand, in the early seventies.

Enjoy this excerpt from his book, *The Leadership Files*, volume 1

QUALITY FOCUS

"Whatever things are true, noble, just, pure, lovely, good report, virtue, anything praiseworthy— meditate on these things." Philippians 4:8
Make your mind dwell on the beautiful, the good, the true, the pure.
Focus on low quality things—you'll develop low quality living.
Focus on high quality subjects—develop a high quality life.
How we see ourselves is what we will become.
What our mind is preoccupied with makes us the kind of people we are.
We conform to the picture in our mind.
What's your focus right now?

art sales
info@philpringlegallery.com

book sales
ccceshop.com.au

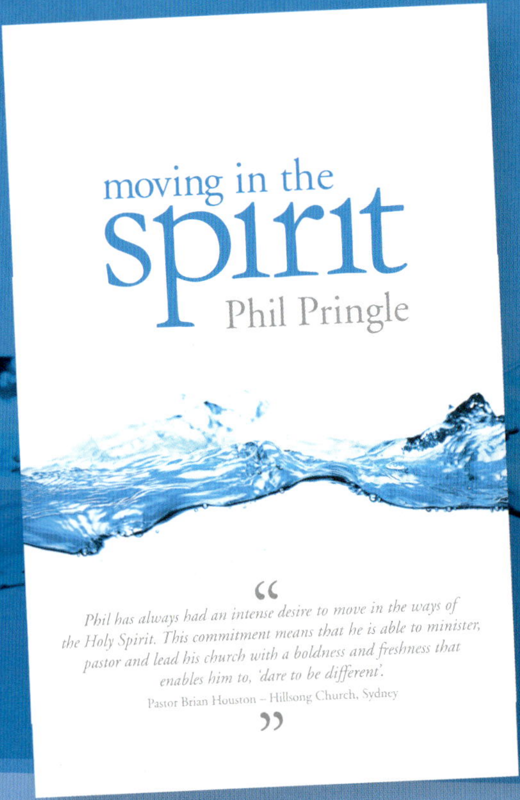

Greater holy power in our lives means greater harvests for God.

This book will help you be more effective in your walk with God by leading you into a closer relationship with the Holy Spirit, the person – not just to teach you about Him, but rather to bring you into connection with Him.

moving in the spirit
Phil Pringle

> "Phil has always had an intense desire to move in the ways of the Holy Spirit. This commitment means that he is able to minister, pastor and lead his church with a boldness and freshness that enables him to, 'dare to be different'."
>
> Pastor Brian Houston – Hillsong Church, Sydney

"I strongly urge you to read this book. The ebb and flow of the Spirit of God is difficult to detect for some, but not for my friend Phil. He is one of the most sensitive ministers to the breath and wind of God I've met."

Pastor Dick Bernal – Jubilee Christian Centre, San Hose

Available at your favorite Christian retailer or online at www.ccceshop.com.au

PAXMinistries

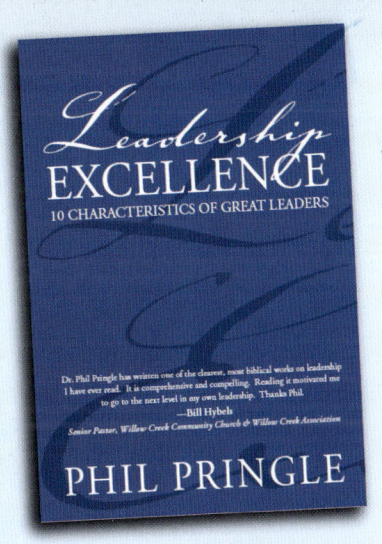

What people are saying about *Leadership Excellence* by Dr. Phil Pringle

I would like to recommend *Leadership Excellence* by Dr. Phil Pringle. All true Christians are called to use their talents and gifts in a position of authority in the body of Christ. This book will help each Christian understand his or her role in the body.
—**Dr. David Yonggi Cho** *The Yoido Full Gospel Church, Seoul, South Korea*

Phil Pringle's outstanding leadership skills have been proven over many years, and so he is well qualified to write this exceptional book on leadership.
—**Pastor Brian Houston** *General Superintendent, Assemblies of God Australia / Senior Minister, Hillsong Church, Sydney, Australia*

Leadership is a hot topic and for good reason—we've never needed good leaders more than today. In a world overrun with principles, ideals, and wish lists about leadership it is refreshing to hear from a practicing, effective, productive, and influential leader. And a leader who isn't driven by the bottom line but by people and their development and well-being. Years of consistency and fruitfulness have penned these pages.

—**Kong Hee** *Senior Minister, City Harvest Church, Singapore*

PAX Ministries

Available at your favorite Christian retailer or online at www.ccceshop.com.au

"Safe in angels arms, far from here, our children run and play…"

Jesse: Found in Heaven will bring hope and comfort to every family suffering the loss of a baby or child.

> What a beautiful treasure this book has been in my life and the lives of those I have shared it with. Jesse: Found In Heaven has touched a place deep in my heart personally and has created a greater anticipation for the wonder and beauty of what we will encounter when we are reunited with our little loved ones in heaven. What joy!

Helen Burns
Senior Pastor, Victory Christian Centre, Vancouver BC
TV Presenter "Pure Sex and Relationships"
CH 10 Vancouver BC

Video and Audio CD also available.

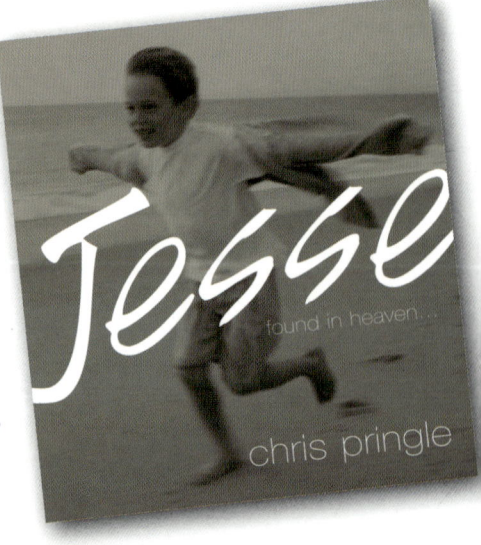

Visit www.jessefoundinheaven.com

Available at your favorite Christian retailer or online at www.ccceshop.com.au

PAX Ministries